The New Gender Paradox

The New Gender Paradox

Fragmentation and Persistence of the Binary

Judith Lorber

polity

First published in 2022 by Polity Press

Polity Press
65 Bridge Street
Cambridge CB2 1UR, UK

Polity Press
101 Station Landing
Suite 300
Medford, MA 02155, USA

ISBN-13: 978-1-5095-4435-6
ISBN-13: 978-1-5095-4436-3(pb)

A catalogue record for this book is available from the British Library.

Library of Congress Control Number: 2021938629

Typeset in 11.5 on 14pt Sabon
by Fakenham Prepress Solutions, Fakenham, Norfolk NR21 8NL
Printed and bound in Great Britain by CPI Group (UK) Ltd, Croydon

For further information on Polity, visit our website:
politybooks.com

Contents

Acknowledgments

I want to thank Jonathan Skerrett, Polity editor, for suggesting this book. I'd also like to thank Susan Farrell, Kathleen Gerson, and Patricia Yancey Martin for their reviews at various stages and the anonymous reviewers of the first draft for their astute comments. Much of the book was written during the various levels of the COVID-19 lockdowns. That should have given me the gift of time, but anxiety over the pandemic often ate away at my ability to concentrate and write. I thank friends and East End Temple Sisterhood members for their psychological support.

The inspiration for the book came from J. Lorber (2018), "Paradoxes of Gender Redux: Multiple Genders and the Persistence of the Binary," in J. W. Messerschmidt, P. Y. Martin, M. A. Messner, and R. Connell (eds), *Gender Reckonings: New Social Theory and Research*, New York: New York University Press.

Some material in the book is adapted from J. Lorber (2005), *Breaking the Bowls: Degendering and Feminist Change*, New York: W. W. Norton, and these articles and reviews: "Using Gender to Undo Gender: A Feminist Degendering Movement," *Feminist Theory* 1 (2000): 101–18; "Constructing Gender: The Dancer and the Dance," in J. A. Holstein and J. F. Gubrium (eds), *Handbook of Constructionist Research*, New York: Guilford Publications, (2008); "Review Essay: Gendered and Sexed Brains,"' *Contemporary Sociology* 40 (2011): 405–9; "Review Essay: Why Do Bathrooms Matter?," *Contemporary Sociology* 41 (2012): 598–602.

New York
March 31, 2021

Introduction

Recently, I received an email urging everyone to use gender-neutral pronouns – they, their, them. A longtime proponent of doing away with gender, I nonetheless found myself resisting the erasure of my identity as a woman, even at the cost of maintaining the gender binary that I believed was the source of women's oppression. So I refused. I want to be identified as a woman – she, hers, her. I want women to be visible. Others responded similarly to the email and to an article in *Scientific American* (Saguy and Williams 2019a), especially women of color. They noted the need for visibility and recognition of accomplishments as well as identifying continued areas of discrimination (Hanna et al. 2019). At that point, I realized that one of the reasons for the persistence of the gender binary is the necessity of the continued valorization of women, especially those of denigrated groups.

Today, in western countries, we are seeing both the fragmentation of the gender binary (the division of the social world into two and only two genders) and its persistence. Multiple genders, gender-neutral pronouns and bathrooms, X designations on official documents and other manifestations of degendering are increasingly prevalent, and yet the two-gender structure of most social worlds persists.

The main gender paradox I explored over twenty-five years ago in *Paradoxes of Gender* (Lorber 1994) focused on the rhetoric of gender equality made meaningless by a total system that rendered women unequal and exploited. Today's new gender paradox is a rhetoric of gender multiplicity undermined by a continuing bi-gendered social structure that supports continued gender inequality. Underneath the seeming erasure of a rigid gender binary and its discriminatory norms lurks the persistence of men's power and patriarchal privilege.

When the concept of gender emerged in the early 1970s, it presented a contrast with the prevailing belief in the biological underpinnings of the behavior of women and men. The concept of gender in this book rests on social construction – the contention that gender differences are made through socialization of children and maintained through surveillance of adults (West and Zimmerman 1987). The norms of a binary society coalesce into a gender regime supported by familiar interaction and legal strictures.

People construct gender for themselves and those they interact with by doing or performing gender. These processes institutionalize as gender structures (Martin 2004). Gender as process and structure are both complementary and in conflict. They are complementary in that process creates and maintains structures. They are in conflict because structuration delimits process. With the simultaneous fragmentation and persistence of the gender binary, process is not changing structure.

Politically, gender fragmented long before the current

popularity of multiple genders. Under liberal feminism in the 1970s, the pressure was to treat women and men alike. In order to do so, women were allowed and encouraged to enter men's professions, such as law and medicine, and to run for political office. Today, in the United States, the ceilings still being broken by women include space travel, combat, and being elected president. Other countries have chosen women heads of state.

The problem with this route to gender equality was that women were emulating men but men were not emulating women. [The unspoken implication of gender neutrality was that women deserved the rights and privileges men had as long as they acted like men] (Mackinnon 1987; Saguy, Williams, and Rees 2020). On the other hand, many of the most successful legal cases in the United States gave men rights, such as child custody, without their having to demonstrate women's capabilities.

The counterargument to women's perfect equality with men was to focus on women's special qualities, particularly nurturance and emotional empathy. Women's bodies and sexualities, which had been downplayed by liberal feminism, came to the fore. Radical feminism valorized women's behavior and experiences and, in women's studies, explored women's history and sources of oppression in different gender regimes. Politically, the focus was on women rather than gender per se.

It soon became clear that women were not a global category of people. Intersectionality broke them up by racial and ethnic identity, social class, occupation, sexuality, relationship status, place of residence, age, bodily integrity, and so on. Each of these groups of women had its own political battles to fight, some of which involved allying with the men of their group rather than always envisaging them as the enemy. (See Lorber 2012 for a review of feminist theory and politics.)

In addition to intersectional fragmentation of gender, people today are finding different ways of doing gender, further fragmenting the binary. Multiple genders may seem revolutionary, but they are not changing the binary structure of most gender regimes. They are personal identities, not legal or bureaucratic statuses. Politically, their individualistic rebelliousness does not encourage a unified gender-resistant movement (Lorber 2018). The binary persists and is bolstered by much normative gendered behavior.

After a review of the premises of the social construction of gender, this book will explore both sides of the current paradox of gender – processes in the fragmentation of gender that are undermining the binary and processes in the performance of gender that reinforce the binary's persistence. After that, I'll explore why we aren't having a gender revolution.

My focus and sources are mostly western societies with relatively egalitarian and individualistic gender regimes. Looking at similar issues in societies with different gender regimes would of necessity find different imbalances between fragmentation and persistence of binary genders.

Terms

While there are many variations in nomenclature, the terms I will be using are:

SEX – referring to internal and external anatomy, hormones, chromosomes, and variations of each.

Terms are *male, female, intersex (having mixtures of the biological components of sex)*.

SEXUALITY – referring to physical attraction and sexual behaviors, emotional involvement, relationships. Terms are *heterosexual, homosexual, lesbian, gay, bisexual, asexual*.

GENDER – referring to identity, self-presentation, performance, legal status. Terms are *man, woman, cisgender (gender identity assigned at birth), transgender man (man assigned female at birth), transgender woman (woman assigned male at birth), non-binary (no gender), genderqueer (neither woman nor man, various combinations of gender presentation)*.

1

How Gendered People, Organizations, and Societies Are Constructed

We live in a world that is divided by gender in every way. Gender is a constant part of who and what we are, how others treat us, and our general standing in society. Our bodies, personalities, and ways of thinking, acting, and feeling are gendered. Because we are gendered from birth by naming, clothing, and interaction with family, teachers, and peers, our identity as a boy or girl, and then as a man or woman, is felt as, and usually explained as, a natural outcome of the appearance of our genitalia, the signs of our biological sex. The assumption is that it is biology that produces two social categories of different people, "females" and "males," and that it is inevitable that societies will be divided along the lines of these two categories and that the people in those categories will be different.

It's a twentieth-century *doxa* – that which "*goes without saying because it comes without saying*" (Bourdieu 1977: 167; emphasis in original). Despite its taken-for-grantedness, the search for the biological sources of gender differences fuels the glut of scientific studies on genetic, hormonal, or other physiological origins for all sorts of gendered behavior (Jordan-Young 2010; Van den Wijngaard 1997). Actually, there are very few gender differences, as meta-analyses of compilations of those studies has shown. One research team (Zell, Krizan, and Teeter 2015) had 106 meta-analyses, incorporating data from 12 million people. Most of the gender differences they found were small, with few that were medium (11.9%), large (1.8%), or very large in size (0.8%).

Yet we live in societies structured by gender differences, so, since they are not natural, they need to be constructed. Gender divides people into contrasting social categories, "girls" and "boys" and "women" and "men." In this structural conceptualization, gendering is the process and the gendered social order the product of social construction. Through interaction with caretakers, socialization in childhood, peer pressure in adolescence, and gendered work and family roles, people are divided into two groups and made to be different in behavior, attitudes, and emotions. The content of the differences depends on the society's current culture, values, economic and family structure, and past history. The resultant gendered social order is based on and maintains these differences. Thus there is a continuous loop-back effect between gendered social institutions and the social construction of gender by individuals (West and Zimmerman 1987). In societies with other major social divisions, such as race, ethnicity, religion, and social class, gender is intricately intertwined with these other statuses (West and Fenstermaker 1995). Despite these crosscutting statuses, the contemporary western world is a very bi-gendered world, consisting of only two legal categories – "female" and "male."

For individuals, gender is a major social status that is

intersected with other major social statuses (racial and ethnic group, social class, religion, sexual orientation, etc.) and so gender is actually not a binary status, even though it is treated as such legally, socially, and in most social science research. On an individual basis, gender fragments; from a societal perspective, gender overrides these multiplicities and simply divides people into two categories.

The binary divisions of gender are deeply rooted in every aspect of social life and social organization in most societies. Although the binary principle of gender remains the same, its content changes as other major aspects of the social order change. The gendered division of work has shifted with changing means of producing food and other goods, which in turn modify patterns of childcare and family structures. Gendered power imbalances, which are usually based on the ability to amass and distribute material resources, change with rules about property ownership and inheritance. Men's domination of women has not been the same throughout time and place, but varies with political, economic, and family structures. In the sense of an underlying principle of how people are categorized and valued, gender is differently constructed throughout the world and throughout history. The prevailing tenet is that men dominate women, although the extent of domination fluctuates.

As pervasive as gender is, because it is constructed and maintained through daily interaction, it can be resisted and reshaped by gender troublemakers (Butler 1990). The social construction perspective argues that people create their social realities and identities, including their gender, through their interactions with others – their families, friends, colleagues. Gender is a constant performance, but its enactment is hemmed in by the general rules of social life, cultural expectations, workplace norms, and laws. These social restraints are also amenable to change, but not easily, because the social order is structured for stability (Giddens 1984). Many aspects of gender have been changed through individual agency, group pressure, and social movements. But the underlying binary structure has not.

Gender is built into the western world's overall social system, interpenetrating the production of goods and services, kinship and family, sexuality, emotional relationships, and the minutiae of daily life. Gendered practices have been questioned, but the overall legitimacy of the gendered social order is deeply ingrained and currently bolstered by scientific studies on supposed inborn differences between females and males. The ultimate touchstone is pregnancy and childbirth. Procreative and other biological differences are part of the constructed gendered social order, which is so pervasive that the behavior and attitudes it produces are perceived as natural, including women's greater predisposition to nurturance and bonding. This belief in natural – and thus necessary – differences legitimates many gender inequalities and exploitations of women.

As the concept of gender has developed in the social sciences, it has moved from an attribute of individuals that produces effects in the phenomenon under study (e.g., men's and women's crime rates, voting patterns, labor force participation) to a major building block in the social order and an integral element in every aspect of social life (e.g., how crime is conceptualized and categorized is gendered, political power is gendered, the economy and the labor force are gender-segregated and gender-stratified). Feminist social scientists have mapped out the effects of gendering on daily lives and on social institutions and have produced reams of data on how these processes maintain inequality between women and men.

Feminist theories have linked gendered social structures with gendered personalities and consciousness. Nancy Chodorow (1978) links the division of parenting in the heterogendered western nuclear family to the objectification and emotional repression in men's psyches and the emotional openness and nurturance of women's psyches. Both emerge from the primacy of women in parenting. Boys' separation from their mothers and identification with their fathers and other men leads to their entrance into the dominant world but also necessitates continuous repression of their emotional longings for their mothers and fear of castration. Girls' continued identification with their mothers makes them available for intimacy; their heterosexual coupling with emotionally dissatisfying men produces their desires to become mothers and reproduces the gendered family structure from which gendered psyches emerge.

As for the sources of women's oppression, multicultural and postcolonial feminists claim that there are complex systems of dominance and subordination, in which some men are subordinate to other men, and to some women as well (Collins 2000; Trinh 1989). All men may have a "patriarchal dividend" of privilege and entitlement to women's labor, sexuality, and emotions, but some men additionally have the privileges of whiteness, education, prosperity, and prestige (Connell 1995). A gender analysis sees gender hierarchies as inextricable from other hierarchies, but conversely argues that hierarchies of class, race, and achievement must be seen as substantively gendered (Acker 1999; Glenn 1999). In this sense, difference is expanded from men versus women to the multiplicities of sameness and difference among women and among men and within individuals as well, these differences arising from similar and different social locations (Braidotti 1994; Felski 1997; Frye 1996).

Despite these intersecting multiplicities, the western social world is divided into only two genders, and the members of each of these categories are made similar enough to be easily identifiable and different enough from the members of the other category to be allocated separate work and family responsibilities, and to be economically rewarded and culturally valued in significantly non-equivalent ways.

Social constructionist structural feminist theory argues that the gendered social order is constantly restabilized even when disrupted by individual and collective action, while postmodern feminism has shown how individuals can consciously and purposefully create disorder and categorical instability, opening the way to change (Flax 1987). The social order is an intersectional structure, with socially constructed individuals and groups ranged in a pyramidal hierarchy of power and powerlessness, privilege and disadvantage, normality and otherness. Because these social statuses and the rationales that legitimate their inequality are constructed in the interaction of everyday life and in cultural representations and solidified in institutional practices and laws, they can all be subverted by resistance, rebellion, and concerted political action.

But most people do gender all the time, usually without thinking. Whether they are privileged or oppressed, people do gender because not to do so is to be shamed as unmanly or unwomanly. In this dual sense of doing and done to lies the power of gender as a socially constructed system of inequality. This power is enormously strengthened by the invisibility of gender processes, the lack of reflection in doing gender, and the belief that the gender order is based on natural and immutable sex differences.

This bi-gendered social structure is what is currently being fragmented in multiple ways – by choosers of non-binary identities and those who queer or question its foundations and by transgender people who may straddle traditional understandings of women's and men's identities, by intersex activists and athletes, and by those erasing gendered language use. At the same time, bi-gendering is being upheld by beliefs in the biological source of gendered brains and behavior, research based on only two gender categories, standpoint stances that valorize women, hegemonic masculinity, the #MeToo movement, gender-based violence, and sexualities dependent on gendered partners.

Ethnomethodological insights into gender construction

Gender as a construct first appeared in Harold Garfinkel's *Studies in Ethnomethodology* (1967) in the story of Agnes. Agnes was a 19-year-old with fully developed breasts, penis, and testicles who came to a UCLA center for the study of people with "severe anatomical irregularities." She presented as intersexual but in actuality was a normal boy who had been taking female hormone pills stolen from her mother since the age of twelve. What was important to Garfinkel was the way that Agnes achieved the gender display of a "natural, normal female" through voice pitch, gestures, dress, and other mannerisms that today we would call "emphasized femininity." We never hear from Agnes, but the construction of gender identity by transgender people has subsequently been described in many of their own accounts and is now a staple of the constructionist literature (Bolin 1988; Devor 1997; Ekins 1997).

Buried in Garfinkel but subsequently spotlighted by gender studies analysts is the idea that it is not only transgender individuals who create a gender identity; everyone produces a version of masculinity or femininity socially and culturally acceptable enough to meet the expectations of normality in the eyes of others in their social groups. Building on Garfinkel, Suzanne Kessler and Wendy McKenna, in *Gender: An Ethnomethodological Approach* (1978), showed that gender is produced as a social fact by presenting a self that is acceptable to others. Gender attribution reproduces the gender binary by ignoring anomalies and assuming anatomical congruence with outer appearance. Genitalia may be the signs used in the initial assignment of an infant to a sex category, but in gender attribution, the genitalia under clothing are assumed; Kessler and McKenna call them "cultural." In their ethnomethodological account of gender construction, Kessler and McKenna focus on the role of the "other" in the validation of gender, but they end their book by coming back to the doer: "All persons create both the reality of their specific gender and a sense of its history, thus at the same time creating the reality of two, and only two, natural genders" (1978: 139).

Garfinkel did not address the question of the extent of consciousness and complicity in the construction of gender because he did not know until years after that Agnes had been lying about the source of her bodily anomalies (breasts and a penis). In a feminist re-analysis of the story of Agnes, Mary Rogers (1992) argued that Garfinkel was an unwitting "gender collaborator" who displayed the masculinity Agnes needed as a contrast.

Although most cisgender people present themselves as women or men without the deliberate impression management of transgender people, there were times when Garfinkel was well aware that he played up to Agnes's emphasized femininity by a complementarily emphasized masculinity – holding doors open, seating her in a car, and so on. What were below the surface of his awareness, according to Rogers, were the power differentials in his relationship with Agnes. He was older, a professional, in control of the interview sessions, and with the other men in the research/clinic situation, the ultimate decider of whether Agnes would get the sex-change surgery she desired. And so, like other western women in the 1950s, Agnes had to be manipulative and secretive to get what she wanted from men who had power over her.

Constructionist feminist theory and research subsequently focused on how girls and women consciously learn heterosexual gender displays and subservient behavior as strategies to attract a husband, but seemed to assume that boys and men absorbed the attitudes of patriarchal privilege much less consciously. Since consciousness raising was at one time a radical feminist political strategy, it would seem that without the "click" of self-awareness, women are no more conscious of the gender construction of their lives than men are.

The use of Agnes in the feminist literature as a model of the production of femininity by "normal, natural females" greatly expanded the concept of gender construction. A huge body of empirical research shows how girls and women in western societies are made docile, submissive, emotional, and nurturant through socialization by parents, teachers, peers, and imitation of constantly presented media depictions of heterosexual attractiveness. Later work on masculinity shows that the same process takes place in the making of assertive, emotionally repressed, sexually aggressive boys and men, with the addition of sports as an arena for reward and emulation of violent behavior (Messner 2002).

Doing gender

The signature term in constructionist gender studies is "doing gender." West and Zimmerman argued that:

> gender is not a set of traits, not a variable, nor a role, but the product of social doings of some sort. . . . Doing gender means creating differences between girls and boys and women and men, differences that are not natural, essential, or biological. Once the differences have been constructed, they are used to reinforce the "essentialness" of gender. (1987: 129, 137)

Given membership in a sex category, doing gender is inevitable and unavoidable in a gendered society. One's gender performance is evaluated by others and one is accountable for its appropriateness. The end result is not only personal and interpersonal gendering, but gendered workplaces, politics, medical and legal systems, religions, and cultural productions: "Doing gender furnishes the interactional scaffolding of social structure, along with built-in mechanisms of social control" (1987: 147).

To the extent that women conform to norms of femininity, they are complicit in their own oppression, just as men who benefit from the privileges of masculinity are complicit in reproducing that oppression (Martin 2001, 2003). The pressures of accountability for doing gender properly create family–work conflicts among successful women (Blair-Loy 2003; Hochschild 1997). These pressures constrain their career and family choices in ways that are often not of their own choosing. The discourse shaping the norms of work and family reflects invidious gendered assumptions and values. Julia Nentwich (2004), a Swiss psychologist, suggests alternative language to construct different realities. Within a work organization, she says, women can be different – exotic, not the norm, a problem to integrate. Or they can be similar, so that treating them differently is discrimination. In the family, the language of the traditional division of labor puts children and jobs in conflict, makes a paid job a privilege for mothers and spending time with the family a privilege for fathers. In contrast, the language of equal partnership assumes that her paid work is important to the woman, that fathers take care of their children, and that both participate in work and family. On full-time versus part-time work, the dominant language framework is that full-time has to be the norm because the demands of the job come first, performance is measured by time spent at the job, and work and private life are two separate spheres. In an alternative language framework, performance is measured by fulfilling objectives, jobs can be partitioned, and work, family, and other life concerns are overlapping spheres (Epstein et al. 1999).

Gender as performativity

If "doing gender" has been the touchstone of gender construction in the social sciences, Judith Butler's concept of *performativity*, from *Gender Trouble* (1990), has been the prevailing concept in the humanities. Conceptually based in philosophy and psychoanalytic theory, Butler's concept of performativity encompasses the unconscious process of making gendered selves that reiterate social norms of femininity and masculinity and inscribe femaleness and maleness on the body and heterosexuality on the psyche. Performance and identity are one and the same; one does not precede or exist without the other. And there lies the possibility for "gender trouble." Gendering has to be done over and over, almost ritualistically, to reproduce the gendered social norms. But different ways of gendering produce differently gendered people. So, with conscious deliberation, one might create oneself differently gendered, and indeed, transgender people do just that. By 1993, Butler was rethinking aspects of gender performativity. In *Bodies That Matter* (1993), she took up the materiality or bodiedness of gender performativity and analyzed the ways that it encompassed sex and sexuality as well.

Butler ended *Gender Trouble* by arguing for the subversive political possibilities inherent in gender performativity. She said, "The loss of gender norms would have the effect of proliferating gender configurations, destabilizing substantive identity, and depriving the naturalizing narratives of compulsory heterosexuality of their central protagonists: "man" and "woman"" (1990: 146).

Constructing gendered structures

Structuration is the congealing of the situationally based rules of interactive processes and practices and their enforced application across time and space (Giddens 1984). Concepts of gendered organizations, gender regimes, and gender as an institution convey stability and solidity, in contrast to the fluidity and mutability of doing gender and gender performativity. Gendered structures are not just the accumulation of gender processes; they constitute and organize a major part of the social order. With structuring, gendered practices (process) are imposed on by institutionalized patterns of social interaction embedded in legal and bureaucratic rules and regulations. Most significantly, these institutionalized patterns are imbued with domination and power.

A prime arena for research on gender structuration is the organization of workplaces (Acker 1990; Britton 2000; Ferguson 1984). A workplace is more or less structurally gendered on several levels. One is the extent of the division into women's and men's jobs; another is the steepness or flatness of the hierarchy of authority and prestige and the gender clustering at each level; still another is the range of wage and benefits scales and where women and men workers fall on it. The extent of gendering depends on the decisions, policies, and history of the particular workplace, which reflect and reproduce its structure through the interactions of workers as colleagues, bosses, and subordinates.

When workers are recruited to a heavily gendered workplace, a belief in the importance of gendered characteristics influences the search for candidates who are "masculine" or "feminine." In westernized cultures, "masculine" traits would be rationality, objectivity, and aggressiveness; "feminine" traits would be emotional sensitivity, psychological perceptivity, and ability to mediate and compromise. In a non-gendered workplace, the search would be for workers who exhibited "neutral" characteristics, such as intelligence, honesty, experience, and mental agility. The gender designations of attributes as masculine, feminine, or neutral are culturally contingent, and the skills needed for a job are frequently re-gendered as the gender composition of the workforce changes (Jacobs 1989; Reskin and Roos 1990). The same jobs can be stereotyped as masculine "dangerous work" in one country and feminine work needing "nimble fingers" in another (Poster 2001).

The end result of the attribution of desired characteristics is the valuation of men workers over women workers, men's jobs over women's jobs, and "masculine" over "feminine" work capabilities. However the workplace is gendered, the economic outcome seems to be stubbornly uniform in advantaging men. Salaries are highest in jobs where men are the predominant workers, whether the worker is a woman or a man, and lowest in jobs where women are the predominant workers, again whether the worker is a man or a woman. Looked at from the perspective of the worker, men have the advantage no matter what the gender composition of the job or workplace since they earn more than women in jobs where men are the majority, in jobs where women are the majority, and in gender-balanced jobs.

The pervasive cultural beliefs about women and men workers that perpetuate gender inequality support the devaluation of women's competence by men. Women themselves help to sustain the devaluation because they frequently compare themselves with other women, not men, at the same level. The unequal salary scales and opportunities for career advancement thus seem fair because there are no challenges to the beliefs that sustain them. In sum, the process producing gender inequality in the workplace is both interactive and structural. As Cecilia Ridgeway (1997) says, "The result is a system of interdependent effects that are everywhere and nowhere because they develop through multiple workplace interactions, often in taken-for-granted ways. Their aggregate result is structural: the preservation of wage inequality and the sex segregation of jobs" (1997: 230).

Gender regimes

Gender structures nation-states into gender regimes. Just as organizations are not aggregates of gendered practices but have a logic of their own, gender regimes are not aggregations of gendered organizations. Gender regimes stratify women and men across organizations, so that they are valued more or less over a matrix of statuses that determine their access to power, prestige, and economic resources (Collins 2000; Yuval-Davis 1997). Commonly, gender intertwines with racial, ethnic, and class stratification, so that gender is only one aspect of an intersectional complex of inequality (Acker 2006; Collins 2019; Crenshaw 1989; McCall 2001).

Many gender regimes privilege one group of men. In *Masculinities*, Connell (1995) contrasted hegemonic men and subordinated men. Hegemonic men have economic and educational advantages and institutionalized patriarchal privileges, and their characteristics are the most valued attributes of masculinity. Subordinated men are not necessarily devalued, but they have fewer opportunities for advancement and little of the power, prestige, and wealth of hegemonic men. Connell describes how the values of western hegemonic masculinity are produced through college education, where young men are trained to be rational and technically expert, and reproduced in professional and managerial careers in hierarchically organized workplaces, where hegemonic men expect eventually to have positions of authority over other men. Which men are hegemonic and which subordinated shifts with changing historical conditions but, according to Connell, the hegemony of white European masculinity over the past 500 years has spread globally through colonization, economic control, and state violence (Connell 1993, 1998, 2005).

Gender as a social institution

According to Giddens, society-wide structural principles that extend over time and space can be considered *institutions* (1984). In *Paradoxes of Gender* (1994), I claimed that gender was a social institution based on three structural principles: the division of people into two social groups, "men" and "women," the social construction of perceptible differences between them, and their differential treatment legitimated by the socially produced differences. In complex societies, the binary division by gender overrides individual differences and intertwines with other major social statuses – racial categorization, ethnic grouping, economic class, age, religion, and sexual orientation – to create a hierarchical system of dominance and subordination, oppression, and exploitation. The members of the dominant gender status, usually hegemonic men, legitimate and rationalize the gender order through politics, the media, the education system, religion, and the production of knowledge and culture. Gendered kinship statuses reflect and reinforce the prestige and power differences of the different genders and institutionalize heterosexuality as an intrinsic part of gender as a social institution (Butler 2002; Ingraham 2006).

The concept of gender as a social institution makes change seem impossible, but institutions do evolve or are drastically altered through political movements. Through feminist political activism and other political and social forces, the institution of gender has certainly evolved in western societies: Women and men now have formal equality in all the major social spheres (Jackson 1998). No laws prevent women from achieving what they can, and many laws help them do it by preventing discrimination and sexual harassment. More and more countries are ratifying laws to protect women's procreative and sexual rights, and to designate rape, battering, and genital mutilation as human rights crimes. However, despite formal and legal equality, discriminatory treatment of women still regularly occurs in the economy and in politics. Gender equality has not significantly penetrated the family division of labor, and conflicts over who takes care of the children spill over and are exacerbated by gender inequities in the paid job market. Women have not gained the power or economic resources in most western societies to ensure the structural bases of gender equality, and so their successes are constantly being undermined by the vicissitudes of the economy, a war, the resurgence of religious fundamentalism, or a pandemic.

Conclusion

To review: The processes of doing gender and gender performance construct individual identity. Gendered individuals in interaction with others equally gendered construct gendered organizations. These are cemented by a gender-segregated and stratified job market, gendered political structures, family and kinship systems, cultural productions, religions, and educational systems into gendered regimes within which individual constructions of gender play out. It is this edifice of gender that is fragmenting in many ways and being sustained in other ways. The next two chapters will describe these two warring trends.

2
Fragmentation of the Gender Binary

Within the space of two weeks in 2014, the *New York Times* published several pieces on multiple genders. One was on the fifty-some choices of gender identity for Facebook users (Ball 2014; Herbenick and Baldwin 2014). The conclusion was that the gender binary was breaking up and that was a good thing. Actually, the idea of using multiple genders to fragment the binary is not new. In 1995, Sandra Bem, a long-time proponent of abolishing gender, proposed that "rather than trying to dismantle the two-and-only-twoness of gender polarization and compulsory heterosexuality by *eliminating* gender categories, we instead dismantle that two-and-only-twoness by *exploding* or *proliferating* gender categories" (1995: 330; italics in original).

The effect is not only to multiply possibilities and recognition of multiple sexes, sexualities, and genders, but to destroy the concept of oppositeness and its implicit designations of normality and deviance.

In addition to multiple gendering, there are other current manifestations of the fragmentation of the gender binary. Other ways the gender binary is being broken up that I will discuss in this chapter are: multi-gender bathrooms, intersex identities and intersex athletes, transgender men (female-to-male) who continue to menstruate and who become pregnant and give birth, non-gendered pronouns and language, and doing research without the binary. I will end with the pros and cons of fragmenting the binary.

Multiple genders

Some of the variant gender identities are bi-gender, agender, gender fluid, questioning, queer, trans man, trans woman, intersex, neutrois, two-spirit, and variations of each. Australia's High Court has allowed someone to register their gender officially as "nonspecific" (Baird 2014). India's Supreme Court recognized transgender as a third gender (Varma and Najar 2014). Germany allows parents of intersexed babies to register them as "indeterminate" (Nandi 2013). "Queer," once a radical identity, has almost become the new normal (Wortham 2016). These are twenty-first-century iterations of going beyond the binary, the strict division of people into two and only two sexes and genders.

The most radical among the gender variations is non-binary, trying to live entirely outside the gender structure. A survey of 27,715 transgender people in the United States reported that non-binary people may account for 25–35 percent of the transgender population; they reside predominantly in metropolitan areas (James et al. 2016). Estimates of the number of people in the general population of the United States and the United Kingdom who define themselves as non-binary fluctuate with the definition of non-binary (Richards et al. 2017).

A non-binary Wiki was created in 2017 with 410 content pages and 1,224 registered users. It has a blog for an annual survey of "humans worldwide whose genders or lack thereof are not fully described by the gender binary." The 2019 gender census had 11,242 responses (Lodge 2019). The most popular answers to the question, "Which of the following best describe(s) in English how you think of yourself?", broke down to: non-binary – 66.6%, queer – 43.0%, trans –36.6%, enby – 31.7%, transgender – 30.4%. (Choices were multiple.) The choices of titles were: no title at all – 33.0%, Mx – 31.3%, Mr – 8.7%, non-gendered prof./acad. – 5.5%, Ms – 4.7%. The choices of pronouns were: singular they/them/their/theirs/themself – 79.5%, he/him/his/himself – 30.8%, she/her/hers/herself – 29.0%, none/avoid pronouns – 10.3%, xe/xem/xyr/xyrs/xemself – 7.2%. It's clear from this survey that there isn't a consensus among those who identify as non-binary for designation, titles, or pronouns with the somewhat contradictory choices of gendered titles and pronouns.

Helena Darwin (2017) found that on the Reddit genderqueer subgroup there were those who identified as "agender, aliagender, androgynous, bi-gender, demigirl/demiguy, genderfluid, genderflux, genderfuck, gender variant, intergender, neutrois, poly-gender, and pangender" (315). Other variations are in the presentation of self – "doing non-binary." In an interview study of 47 non-binary people, Darwin (2020) found much blurring between non-binary and transgender. Darwin concludes that "the non-binary identity category functions as an umbrella for a host of gender identities" (2017: 331). Ironically, if non-binary is thought of as another category of gender, it remains in the gender regime (Barbee and Schrock 2019: 576).

Another variation is people who are asexual and also agender. The two are not automatically linked; asexuality is described as non-chosen, agender as a deliberately adopted identity (Cuthbert 2019). The rationale, according to 12 out of the 21 interviewees in this study, is that sexuality needs opposite genders, and since they were asexual it made sense to them to be agender. It was also a way to stop being identified as a sexual target. The overlap between asexuality and agender is a minority position. In the 2016 Asexual Community Census, 26 percent of asexual respondents (2,420 out of 9,294) identified as non-binary, agender, genderqueer or similar options (Bauer et al. 2018).

On surveys, people tend not to identify as transgender when it is one of several categories. Increasingly, a two-step technique is used: Respondents are asked to identify their sex attribution at birth and their current gender identity (Saperstein and Westbrook 2021). Less used but providing accurate data are to place oneself on a gradient of woman to man with non-binary at the center, and also to identify one's self-presentation and perception by others on a gradient ranging from feminine to masculine.

A recent study of 17 non-binary interviewees found that all reported emotional exhaustion in the battle for acceptance as non-gendered (Barbee and Schrock 2019). Most interviewees were between 18 and 23 years old, three were 29–35 and one was 63. Eleven were white, three identified as Latinx, two as South Asian, and one as "mixed." The interviewers were themselves non-binary. Presenting as non-gendered involved clothing, hair (facial and head), voice pitch and manner of talking, pronoun usage, name change, and choice of romantic partner.

Appearance then becomes activism. When challenged

or mis-gendered, non-binary respondents have to explain that genders are constructed and there are more than two, thus constantly educating those they are interacting with. More onerous is the need for vigilance in the face of hostility and potential violence from strangers since gender-mixed appearances often incur open antagonism. As one non-binary respondent said:

> People don't know what to make of me when they see me, because they feel my features contradict one another. They see no room for the curve of my hips to coexist with my facial hair; they desperately want me to be someone they can easily categorise. My existence causes people to question everything they have been taught about gender, which in turn inspires them to question what they know about themselves, and that scares them. Strangers are often desperate to figure out what genitalia I have . . . (Ford 2015)

The emotional benefits were feelings of "authenticity and confidence, pride in problematizing the binary, and liberation from the strictures of binarily gendered clothing and behavioral expectations" (Barbee and Schrock 2019: 589).

The description of the struggles of those who don't want to be identified as a man or a woman suggests that it takes all their psychic strength to live in an often hostile binary world (Bergner 2019). It would be hard to negotiate the psychological and interpersonal obstacles and mount a battle with gendered laws and policies at the same time. As a result, non-binary people's potential structural challenge to the binary system disappears.

In many ways, the existence of non-binary and queer identities is in itself revolutionary (Nicholas and Clark 2020). However, the individuality of the adoption of an alternate gender forecloses the possibility of a non-binary movement. Gender goes back to being a personal identity, even though many of the battles have to be fought with bureaucracies and legal policies.

Gender-neutral bathrooms

The "bathroom wars" are a clear case of how multiple gendering clashes with state policies of gender. The demand for gender-neutral bathrooms used to come from feminist women tired of waiting in long lines while men's rooms were empty. It was an integral part of the fight for gender equality (Molotch 1988). The current demand for gender-neutral bathrooms is coming from people who are gender-variant (Brown 2005; Weiner 2015). In the United States, the demands for gender-neutral bathrooms are still seen as so radical as to continue to warrant legal battles (Liptak 2016; Suk Gersen 2016). In the 2015 US Transgender Survey, nearly 60 percent of respondents reported being too afraid to use public restrooms out of fear of a confrontation and 12 percent reported being verbally harassed while accessing a bathroom in the past year (James et al. 2016).

Gender-variant users of multiple-use bathrooms visibly confront the binary gender social order. They violate what is to many people the psychological and biological immutability of their own sex and gender identity. In *Queering Bathrooms*, Sheila Cavanagh (2010) explored the shocked responses to the use of conventional bathrooms by people whose gender appearance is ambiguous. She suggests that being in a bathroom with someone of a seemingly different gender disrupts the psyche's carefully developed gender identity, achieved in great part through toilet training.

The confrontation challenges the expectation that everyone is the same gender since they were born and have bodies congruent with gender appearance. Cavanagh interviewed 100 mostly white, able-bodied, middle-to-upper-class graduate students and others aged 18–59 who identified as transsexual or transgender, as gender queer, and as gay, lesbian, and bisexual. Three self-identified as intersex. Their experiences were with gender-identified western bathrooms. Many were activists, so they were able to analyze the reaction to their bathroom use. They reported double takes, verbal challenges, calling security guards, and even arrests.

Conventional users of gendered bathrooms uphold the binary and the clear segregation of women and men in certain public spaces. Safety is invoked, although women would be safer in bathrooms where there are several of each gender. The comfort of being with "one's own" in a private space is also an issue. There is no official mandate for non-gendered bathrooms, the way legal racial desegregation and laws governing access for the disabled altered bathroom use in the United States. In "On not making history," Harvey Molotch (2010) described a multi-gendered bathroom that never got built at New York University's new facilities for a Department of Social and Cultural Analysis. He says, "It was a lost opportunity to inscribe social change into architectural form and to use form to facilitate intellectual growth" (264). But it didn't have enough supporters who were willing to fight for it. While discussing the politics of gender-neutral bathrooms on college campuses, Alexander Davis (2020) notes that they can be cultural capital, likely to be introduced if they enhance an institution's marketability.

Intersex identifiers

One group that has become politically active are open intersex identifiers. In *Contesting Intersex*, Georgiann Davis (2015) describes how intersex is currently experienced, defined, and fought over. She is an insider to these debates, as she has an intersex trait (complete androgen insensitivity syndrome) and in 2013 was elected president of the Androgen Insensitivity Syndrome-DSD Support Group. Like many other intersex people, Davis was not told the truth when she was diagnosed at the age of 13 and had irreversible surgery (removal of undescended testes) at 17. She found out about her intersex status at 19, when she saw her medical records and was so upset, she threw them away. Ten years later, she was able to explore her diagnosis and treatment through the lens of feminist gender and sexuality scholarship.

One of the areas of activism that Davis explored is the shift in nomenclature from intersex as a "disorder of sex development" (DSD) to a gender identity. In this sense, intersex goes from an ascribed to a chosen identity.

Davis's interviews with 36 people who have intersex traits revealed two major and oppositional patterns: Those who favored the use of intersex as an identity tended to accept the idea of the social construction of gender and sex and their fluidity and to identify as non-heterosexual (see also Preves 2003). The consequence was confrontations with parents and medical experts over their treatment. Two-thirds of the intersex people Davis interviewed were in this group. The other third accepted the use of DSD even with its emphasis on disorder and the consequent stigma of abnormality. They adhered to an essentialist view of sexuality and gender as binary and hardwired, and they collaborated with parents' and medical experts' recommendations of surgical alterations for the bodily manifestations of their intersex trait. With the surgery, they identified as a woman or man.

These patterns at the individual level of gender were paralleled at the interactional level with parents (17 interviews) and medical experts (10 interviews). Medical experts impose a gender on intersex infants that is based on the appearance of genitalia (Kessler 1990). They then recommend immediate surgical treatment to correct what is now diagnosed as a disorder within a rigid gender binary. With the body "corrected," the child can be raised in a clearly designated gender. Most parents believed that sex and gender were fetally established and immutable, and they accepted the DSD nomenclature. The underlying stigma of abnormality and fear of homosexuality, however, led most parents to hide the diagnosis and lie about the need for treatment – to prevent cancer is the usual rationale.

In her discussion of advocacy organizations, Davis focuses on the shift from "collective confrontation" to "contested collaboration," with acceptance of DSD as the diagnosis. Those organizations which resist the term "disorders" have used "differences of sex development" while other organizations insist that "intersex" is the proper term. However, the question of intersex as an identity has itself created contention, with some intersex advocates rejecting its legal adoption as a "third sex" as stigmatizing.

As an activist, Davis lays out seven "actions for liberation": stop medically unnecessary surgeries, collaborate with medical experts, expand and diversify peer support, empower through education about gender and sex variability, use feminist scholarship on gender construction, understand the institutional construction of diagnoses and other stigmatizing labels, and incorporate children's voices into medical decisions. Intersex liberation could become a direct confrontation with the gender binary if the variations of sex development became variations in gender identity or a legal third gender. But the more common treatment is to "normalize" genitalia and grow up in an "appropriate" gender.

Intersex athletes

In their struggle to maintain clear gender boundaries, sports organizations have targeted hormones and chromosomes, but these don't clearly distinguish female from male. The current focus is on testosterone and its higher-than-normal levels in intersex women athletes, particularly competitive runners.

Major sports organizations set up binary gender borders but come up against multiple variations when they try to use physical anatomy – visible genitalia, internal procreative organs, chromosomes, hormonal output – as markers of gender boundaries. The International Olympic Committee dropped gender verification tests for women in 2000 but then had to confront transgender and intersex athletes. In 2004, it ruled that female and male transgender people could compete in their new gender, provided they had had "appropriate surgery," had completed hormone treatment two years before, and were legally recognized as members of their new gender.

The contested issue then shifted to possible intersex effects, namely, elevated testosterone levels in intersex runners. In 2009, when Caster Semenya, an 18-year-old South African woman, won the 800-meter race at the World Championships in Athletics in Berlin, her womanhood was challenged by one of her competitors, and a gender verification test was called for (Clarey and Kolata 2009). Semenya won the race with a time of 1 minute 55.45 seconds, the best in the world in 2009, beating the defending champion by 2.45 seconds. Her time was not the all-time fastest, yet none of the other champions had to prove they were women. Semenya was described in one news report as having "an unusually developed muscular frame and a deep voice" (Kessel 2009), hardly accurate criteria for gender verification. But trying to develop "simple rules for complex gender realities" presents a major challenge to gender segregation, wrote Alice Dreger, professor of clinical medical humanities and bioethics at Northwestern University (2009). Measuring testosterone levels might give an indication of muscle mass, but testosterone levels aren't a criterion for gender division. Men with low testosterone levels don't compete with women with similar levels; rather, the men are allowed to boost their levels medically. Their gender identity is not questioned.

Most women have natural testosterone levels of 0.12 to 1.79 nanomoles per liter. The typical male range after puberty is 7.7 to 29.4 nanomoles per liter. The current ruling is that intersex women athletes who want to participate in middle-distance women's track events must take hormone-suppressing drugs to reduce testosterone levels below 5 nanomoles per liter for six months before competing, then maintain those lowered levels. After several lawsuits, in 2019 the international Court of Arbitration for Sport (CAS) upheld this regulation. Caster Semenya brought her case against the International Association of Athletics Federations (IAAF), arguing that IAAF's rule is unscientific, unethical, and discriminatory. She lost (Longman 2020).

The CAS panel agreed that the rule is discriminatory, but justified it based on the IAAF's arguments about sex differences and testosterone. Men are, on average across athletic events, 9–12 percent better than women. The IAAF claims that testosterone is the main cause of this difference. Therefore, women with high testosterone levels have an unfair advantage. These claims about testosterone have been challenged on the grounds that the relationship between testosterone and athletic performance is not clear-cut (Jordan-Young and Karkazis 2019). Training, body size, and menstrual cycles are among the myriad other factors that influence athletic performance.

Even more controversial is the question of whether transgender women, who were once men, should compete in women's sports (Brassil and Longman 2020). Regulations vary and often conflict. There is little data on elite transgender women athletes to determine whether they have physiological advantages. Note that as with intersex athletes, it is women's sports that are invariably the source of conflict since transgender men, who were once women, are not thought to be a threat to men's sports.

Acceptance of people with variations of sex characteristics and development without trying to physically normalize them would go a long way to fragment the gender binary. It would undermine the belief that the behavior of women and men is produced by biology and therefore immutable (Lorber 1993).

Menstruating and birthing men

In 1978, Gloria Steinem asked, "What would happen . . . if suddenly, magically, men could menstruate and women could not?... The answer is clear – menstruation would become an enviable, boast-worthy, masculine event" (Steinem 1978: 110). Some transgender men do menstruate, but it is not an affirming experience for them. The problem harks back to the lack of gender-neutral bathrooms. Men's bathrooms do not have supplies of tampons and sanitary napkins the way many women's bathrooms do, nor do they have places to dispose of used "feminine hygiene" items. Menstruation in women is often stigmatizing, rendering them polluting in many cultures. For transgender men who still menstruate, it's doubly stigmatizing, adding psychological disorientation to physical discomfort (Frank 2020). Menstruation challenges trans men's masculinity, so most hide their periods. It was newsworthy when a bearded transgender man posed with women activists, fashion designers, and writers in T-shirts with period-positive slogans in an "I'm On" campaign (Hosie 2018). That was binary breaking, for sure, but in general, transgender men who menstruate are a hidden phenomenon, and so they may queer menstruation (Frank 2020) but they don't affect the gender binary.

More binary breaking are transgender men who become pregnant and give birth. They are frequently described as "the only" but they are not so uncommon. Australian Medicare, one of the few sources of data on transgender men who get pregnant, reports that 55 transgender men gave birth in 2014–15, 44 in 2015–16, 37 in 2016–17, and 22 in 2018–19 (Hook 2019). Yet pregnant men are also not so visible. They report passing as fat men even at full term, attributing this phenomenon to their beards, markers of maleness (Dozier 2005: 305; Hattenstone 2019).

A man giving birth is always newsworthy and usually

reported erroneously as "the first" (Beatie 2008). This description seems to be a way this potentially binary-breaking phenomenon is fitted into the gender binary as an anomaly. Otherwise, they are normalized. A review of 27 news reports on transgender men giving birth from 14 US news media outlets published between 2013 and 2017 found a consistent pattern of normalization (Lampe, Carter, and Sumerau 2019). The trans men's pregnancies and births are described as the same as cisgender biological processes and their parenting as no different from cisgender fathers. The remarkable phenomenon of a body going from female to male but keeping female reproductive capability is not noted.

A meta-synthesis of 14 articles dated from 2012 to 2019 on transgender men's experiences with pregnancy and childbirth showed that they encountered obstacles and hostility from the medical system (Besse, Lampe, and Mann 2020). In trying to conceive, they were faced with the incompatibility of the hormones they used to transition from female to male and those needed for conception. They encountered lack of access to costly assisted reproductive technology as well as difficulty in paying for it. Once pregnant, they had to decide how to juggle a male identity with a growing abdomen. Some passed as overweight men and others went back to a temporary female identity. Those who maintained presentation as a man in name, pronouns and clothing and didn't hide their pregnancy were truly gender resistant. Because of their discomfort with the medical system, many chose nurse midwives for the birth and some opted for home births.

Some transgender men want to flaunt their births. To counteract his invisibility as a pregnant man, a 32-year-old British transgender man, Freddy McConnell, made a movie called *Seahorse* (male seahorses carry the unborn eggs). It documented the reversal of his transition of ten years, getting pregnant with a sperm donor, his pregnancy, and the birth of his son (Hattenstone 2019). McConnell had taken testosterone and had mastectomies when he was 25, but he didn't have a hysterectomy. In the movie, he describes how his body felt when he stopped taking testosterone: "He started having periods again ('I don't like the idea that I've got tampons in my bag,' he winces); his facial hair gets wispier, his hips broaden, his tummy softens and he starts to speak less from his chest and more from his throat." Yet he never altered his chosen identity as a man. However, he was denied being listed as "father" rather than "mother" on the child's birth certificate. The judge defined "mother" as a physical and biological status – the person who is pregnant and gives birth – while Connell defined "father" in its gendered social status (Magra 2020). In both ways – his own gender identity as a man and the legal enforcement of his status as "mother" – the gender binary was confronted. As binary breaking as a man getting pregnant and giving birth is socially, the medical and legal systems focused on his biology and bounced him back to being a woman.

Battle of the pronouns

The one phenomenon that does seem to be fragmenting the binary is the movement to erase gender distinctions from language usage by calling individuals "they, them, theirs," and identifying ethnicity with gender-neutral tags such as Latinx instead of Latino or Latina. Also, Mx is replacing Ms and Mr for some English speakers (Tobia 2015). These gender-neutral designations, originally designed for non-binary, transgender and other gender non-conformists, are being adopted by cisgender people and used in major newspapers and magazines in the United States (Saguy and Williams 2019b). For linguists, "they" was the word of the year and of the decade in 2020, according to the American Dialect Society (Blaylock 2020). There is an International Pronouns Day on the third Wednesday in October, which began in 2018. It gets endorsements by diverse organizations who promise to create grassroots activities around non-gendered pronouns (pronounsday.org).

The use of "they" as a third-person singular gender-neutral pronoun is not new in English literature or informal conversation ("What's their name?"); it has been in use since the Middle Ages (Baron 2020). That may be why there's so little resistance to it although it does make you stop and think.

The use of gender-neutral pronouns has the same effect as other unexpected language use, such as "she" for president in the United States. It produces comprehension disruption or a "surprise." A British study of pronoun use during the 2016 US and 2017 UK elections, both of which had a woman candidate (Hillary Clinton and Theresa May, respectively), found that the use of "she" pronouns produced "massive comprehension disruption" in US readers but none in UK readers (von der Malsburg, Poppels, and Levy 2020). Britain, of course, had already had a woman prime minister, Margaret Thatcher. In the United States, even when the woman was expected to win, "she" pronouns were rarely used; "they" was used instead.

In 2012, Sweden had schoolchildren using the pronoun "hen" and calling each other "friends" (Tagliabue 2012). More revolutionary is the adoption of non-gendered usage for languages that are deeply gendered, such as Spanish, French, Italian, German, and Hebrew. In Argentina in 2019, teenagers began replacing the masculine "o" and feminine "a" endings with the non-gendered "e" (Schmidt 2019). In 2020, the president, Alberto Fernández, publicly joined them, referring to "Argentines" (Politi 2020). The shift in language coincided with the rise of a feminist movement in Argentina centered around a campaign against femicide, the killing of girls and women because of their gender. That campaign, called Ni Una Menos, (Not One Less), bolstered political support for legalizing abortion, a legislative priority for President Fernández. Non-gendering the name of the country was thus transformed into an aspect of the fight for women's rights.

There have been attempts to create non-binary Hebrew to use in place of the standard male and female grammatical categories (Kushner 2019). French and German have been much more resistant to erasing gender distinctions in language use. The French Academy, the guardian of the French language, is vehemently against it, only allowing the feminization of professional titles (Nossiter 2019). German has long used feminine versions of titles and job descriptions. The proposal to substitute an asterisk for all endings was deemed ridiculous by the Association for German Language (Johnson 2019). A petition signed by 100 writers, satirists, and scholars and titled "stop this gender nonsense" called on trade unions, regional authorities, and journalists to keep German gendered.

European languages that are non-gendered, such as Estonian and Finnish, do make life easier for those who are non-binary. However, as one Estonian speaker points out, there are ways to indicate gender so "genderless languages are not the utopia one may imagine. Assumptions about the binary nature of gender and the status of masculinity seem to survive intact, even under genderless language conditions" (Crouch 2018).

The widespread use of he/she and Ms in English went a long way to erase the long-time designation of he/him/his as referring to women as well as men. That is, any group with one or more men in it was referred to as male, the dominant gender. Insisting on "he or she" and "women and men" was a hard-won feminist fight for women's visibility that unfortunately is now being erased by gender-neutral language. However, erasing gender distinctions in language is a stepping stone to gender equality (Liu et al. 2018). If you can't separate people into distinct categories, you can't treat them differently. But gender blurring needs to go much further than gender-neutral pronouns. Every aspect of the presentation of self needs to be non-binary.

Doing research without the gender binary

Feminist researchers start with the assumption that the content and dividing lines for genders, sexes, and sexualities are fluid and intertwined with other major social statuses; thus, there are no "opposites." Even if we use the categories of "women" and "men," we need to recognize people's different racial and ethnic identities, social classes, religions, nationalities, residencies, and occupations. In some research, we need to compare the women and men within these groups. In other research, we need to compare women and men across groups.

The question becomes, who is being compared to whom? Why? What do we want to find out? Even without challenge to the binary, deconstructing gender reveals many possible categories embedded in social experiences and social practices, as does the deconstruction of sexuality, race, ethnicity, and social class. The resultant multiple categories disturb the neat polarity of familiar opposites that assume one dominant and one subordinate group, one normal and one deviant identity, one hegemonic status and one "other."

Multiplying research categories uses several strategies. One strategy is to recognize that gender statuses combined with other major statuses produce many identities in one individual. Another is to acknowledge that individuals belong to many groups. Further, intersectionality produces structural categories in which multiple forms of oppression and discrimination feed on each other. So if you are researching discrimination in women professionals in male-dominated fields, you need categories of Black, Asian, Latina and Caucasian women professionals.

Therefore, it is extremely important to figure out what you want to know before choosing the subjects and variables for comparison. Samples have to be heterogeneous enough to allow for multiple subject categories. The common practice of comparing women and men frequently produces data that are so mixed that it takes another level of analysis to sort out meaningful subject categories. It would be better to start with patterns of behavior derived from data analysis of all subjects and then see the extent to which these patterns create subject categories that can be compared. In the end, the crucial question is, "What do you want to know?"

Pros and cons of fragmenting the gender binary

In evaluating the fragmenting of the binary, we need to look at the effects on individuals, interaction, and legal and bureaucratic structures of each of the ways that the binary is being broken up – multiple genders, gender-neutral bathrooms, intersex identification, intersex athletes, menstruating and birthing men, gender-neutral language, and multiple-gender research.

The existence of multiple genders allows for a variety of gender non-conforming identities or declaring oneself non-binary, without a gender. To live without a gender in a gendered world is almost impossible since everything in one's presentation of self – clothing, head and facial hair, weight and muscular distribution, name, pronouns – proclaims gender. Mixing gender within a self-presentation is gender non-conforming in that attributes won't add up to a consistent gender. In face-to-face interaction, one can have friends and sexual partners who are declared women, men, non-binary, transgender, and other self-designated identities. Formal documents are offering a non-gender choice but legal designations are still likely to be bi-gendered.

A downside is that people with multiple genders have different goals, which hinders concerted political action. On the other hand, a third-group gender identity – X or "other" – blurs these goals. Another downside is that multiple and non-binary gender identifiers have reported encountering hostility and even violence. As long as one's official documents proclaim a gender, it is impossible to be a "non."

As a woman who has "liberated" many men's rooms, gender-neutral bathrooms are all to the good. Not only non-binary individuals need them, every cisgender person who has stood in a long bathroom line appreciates being able to use whatever bathroom is free. Gender-neutral bathrooms also benefit fathers with infants who need diapering since changing tables are not likely to be found in men's bathrooms. Gender-neutral bathrooms are also appreciated by parents of small opposite-gender children, and transgender men who menstruate. The hostility and legal restrictions faced by gender non-conformists who seem to be using the "wrong" bathroom would be minimized if all bathrooms were non-gendered. What would be missed is the chance to have single-gendered space to commune with like-gender friends.

Intersex people who have fought for open and legal identification as intersex appreciate their acceptance. Intersex activism has also helped in the fight against surgical "normalization" procedures. For parents of children with anomalies of sex development who want to bring up a child with a clear conventional gender, and for older children and adults who don't want to be singled out as biologically different, this movement is seen as hurtful. As for intersex athletes who must battle rigidly gendered sports organizations, they are ending up undergoing surgery or hormone treatment to bring their bodies into line with whatever rules and regulations are set as indicating gender normality.

Menstruating and birthing men are exemplars of breaking the binary. They have split physiological sex characteristics from gender identity in startling ways. But transgender men who have given birth as men have not been able to get legal recognition of their status as fathers. In medical facilities, their pregnancies and births lead to their treatment as women.

Menstruating men need to carry their own supplies and hide their disposal if they are using men's bathrooms. During pregnancy, their appearance may let them pass as fat men, but in the act of menstruating or giving birth, their sex supersedes their chosen gender. In short, these men are legally and physically identified by their bodies as female. They are not able to actually fragment the binary. Recently, however, the phrase "pregnant people" is coming into use, recognizing that reproductive rights are for everyone, not just women.

The use of non-gendered pronouns seems to be growing in popularity and in media usage. Many organizations have sessions teaching the proper way to address those who use "they, their, them" as chosen pronouns, and in many circles and families it is considered polite and loving to use non-gendered pronouns. They do not depend on legal ratification, so they can be adopted by anyone who wants gender invisibility. The downside is loss of visibility and recognition of women who achieve in men's domains or men who are primary parents. The parallel movement, non-gendered languages, is more sporadic in acceptance. It also takes more effort and group action to develop non-gendered language forms in deeply gendered languages, such as German, Italian, Spanish, and Hebrew. Once they are developed, it takes more group action to get them used routinely.

Feminist social science has long gone beyond binary gender categories in research, recognizing the ways that other statuses, such as race, ethnicity, social class, and age, intersect gender. Intersectionality prescribes breaking up gender categories by these other relevant statuses. The resultant data on gender inequality will also be intersected by other statuses, so that you will be comparing Black, Hispanic, Asian, and Caucasian women and men on wages in an economic sector or educational attainment. Such findings are more accurate than simple comparisons of women and men, yet multiple-gender or non-binary categories are rarely part of research unless they are the topic of study.

Conclusion

What fragments the binary are X designations on official documents like birth certificates, non-binary and intersex identities, multiple-gender self-presentations, gender-neutral bathrooms, gender-neutral pronoun use, and intersectional research. What seem to but don't fragment the binary are intersex athletes and menstruating and birthing men. There are many ways that the gender binary is being upheld, which I will discuss in the next chapter.

3

Persistence of the Gender Binary

The gender binary will persist if it isn't resisted or rebelled against since it is built into the structure of most societies and major institutions – economy, family, religion, and so on. Feats of women that seem to challenge the binary – space walks, grueling US Marine Corps training, scientific discoveries – paradoxically uphold it. Without the binary and its discriminatory assumptions of women's physical and mental inferiority, these accomplishments would be commonplace. Instead, they are lauded as historical milestones (Davenport and Beachum 2019).

There are, however, specific supports that are rarely questioned. The most common is physical; females and males have different chromosomes, hormones, procreative systems, and body structure. Brains are also assumed to be different. Major differences in behavior and social interaction must necessarily ensue. All the comparative sex and gender research assumes the differences are binary, not divided by other characteristics or spectrums in themselves.

Feminist focus on women's standpoints and the value of women's history and visibility that created women's studies supports the binary. "New" masculinities have not undercut masculine hegemony. In the #MeToo movement, women rebelled against the normality of their sexual exploitation by hegemonic men, and toppled many, but it didn't affect the binary.

The open acceptance of homosexuality is intertwined with continuance of the binary since both heterosexuality and homosexuality are interlocked with the two genders. As modes of different and same-gender attraction, sexuality mostly relies on two distinct genders. But in lifestyle, rather than undercutting heteronormativity, "homonormativity" began to resemble it, with same-gender couples marrying and having children. The underlying gender structure is maintained.

The transgender resurgence, which seems to blur the binary, needs it. Transitioning means constructing a masculine or feminine persona and, for most transgender women and men, successfully passing from the old to the new gender. Without statuses and identities that are seen as opposite, transition from one to the other could not occur.

In this chapter, I will explore each of these ways that the gender binary is strengthened.

The myth of female and male brains

There is an ongoing debate over the distinctness of female and male brains and the effect of brain structure and function on the binary behavior of women and men (del Giudice et al. 2019; Fine, Joel, and Rippon 2019). A persistent claim of biological "hardwiring" is the theory of brain organization. It was based on the administration of testosterone prenatally to a female guinea pig with resultant male mating behavior (Phoenix et al. 1959). The theory was applied to humans in 1967 and soon became textbook knowledge.

Brain organization theory claims that the path to female and male behavior starts with XX and XY chromosomes, which produce estrogen and testosterone respectively. These hormones construct not only the clitoris and vagina, testes and scrotum, but according to the theory also organize the brain's neural substrates into female and male potential for feminine and masculine characteristics and behavior. This potential is supposedly intensified at puberty by the production of additional estrogen and testosterone.

Critiques of this theory note that just as the social environment affects bodies (exercise affects bone mass and menstruation; smoking affects lungs), the human brain itself shows changes from repeated actions of specialized knowledge, experiences, and training, such as in juggling, ballet, and London taxi driving (Rippon 2019). Cabdrivers' knowledge of the map of London gets imprinted on their brains. The changes fade when they retire.

Another argument against the neat binary of brain organization theory is that androgens and estrogens are both masculinizing and feminizing and affect both women and men (Jordan-Young 2010). In addition, the lines between feminine and masculine behavior are blurry and malleable so that there aren't clearly gender-distinguishable characteristics to link back to female and male brains. Social psychological studies show how easily gendered self-perceptions, attitudes, and behavior thought to be inborn can be reinforced, erased, or reversed by subliminal cues, contexts, and other manipulations (Fine 2010). There aren't average female or male brains to compare and contrast. Brains are rather physical mosaics of individual characteristics (Joel and Vikhanski 2019).

In a test of brain patterning in a contested area of gendered ability, researchers mapped neural processes of mathematics in 3-to-10-year-old children (Kersey, Csumitta, and Cantlon 2019). They measured the brain patterns for mathematics of 55 girls and 49 boys with functional magnetic resonance imaging (fMRI) during viewings of mathematics education videos. They found that boys and girls showed equivalent mathematics-related neural responses. That shouldn't have been surprising since another test of early mathematics ability in 50 girls and 47 boys aged 3-to-9-years-old by the same researchers did not show gender differences in mean ability or variance. The researchers conclude that their results are consistent with the Gender Similarities Hypothesis, which argues that boys and girls function similarly in most areas of cognition and that "gender differences in STEM fields in adults are not derived from intrinsic differences in children's brains but likely from a complex environmental origin."

So not only is it difficult to distinguish male from female brains or to confirm the linkage between gendered brains and gendered behavior, there are very few differences between the behaviors of women and men. One set of researchers (Zell, Krizan, and Teeter 2015) did 106 different meta-analyses, incorporating data from 12 million people. The results showed once again that the majority of gender effects were either very small (39.4%) or small (46.1%); relatively few effects were medium (11.9%), large (1.8%), or very large in size (0.8%).

The linkage of brain organization to feminine and masculine behavior is less a demonstrable cause and effect than an attempt to uphold a binary gender structure by arguing for its biological origin. The contention that nature precedes nurture should crumble as women do more and more actions that were considered naturally masculine, such as military combat, space walks, and running governments as premiers and presidents. But the belief in male and female brains persists.

Gendered research

Almost immediately on the outbreak of COVID-19 and the worldwide spread of the coronavirus that causes it, gendered research began. It appeared that men had a higher death rate from COVID-19 than women and were more likely to develop a severe illness (Xiyi et al. 2020). Possible behavioral causes were men's higher rate of smoking and lesser attention to washing hands. Refusal to wear masks was attributed to machismo attitudes (Victor 2020). Other salient factors are pre-existing conditions and gender-segregated occupational exposures (Shattuck-Heidorn, Reiches, and Richardson 2020). One biological theory focused on chromosomes and hormones (Moalem 2020). Women have two X chromosomes which carry 2,000 genes that interact with women's cells. Cells can use genes on one X chromosome to destroy invading viruses, and genes on the other X chromosome to kill infected cells. Also, XX chromosomes produce estrogens, which stimulate immunological responses, while testosterone seems to suppress them. The protective effect of estrogens led to trials of administering them to men and post-menopausal women with COVID-19 (Rabin 2020).

Another branch of research was on the gender effects of the lockdown that kept workers home and school closures that kept children at home. Employers had to adopt flexible work schedules and telecommuting for men and women employees, for which many women have been fighting for years. Another result of the lockdown was the availability of fathers for childcare and home schooling. Where mothers worked outside the home, as medical providers or grocery and pharmacy employees, fathers had to become the main childcarers.

Reports on sharing housework and childcare by heterosexual cohabiting partners working from home were mixed. In one study, men partners claimed to be doing half the homeschooling; their women cohabiters claimed that *they* were doing 80 percent (Miller 2020). Another study of 1,060 US heterosexual couples on their early COVID-19 experiences found an increase in sharing housework from 26 percent to 41 percent; similar results were reported for shared care of children (Carlson, Petts, and Pepin 2020). A report on 4,915 opposite-gender UK parents with children on domestic work, childcare, and work experiences, during April 29 to May 15, 2020, found many inequities (Packham 2020). Mothers were doing more housework and childcare and less paid work. More women than men had lost their jobs, thrusting them into standard domestic gendered roles. A US study of telecommuting heterosexual couples with children found that by April 2020 mothers with children aged 1–12 had cut back their work time by 4.6 hours per week, while fathers had not cut back at all (Collins et al. 2021). A study comparing work at home before and during the pandemic found that fathers benefited more because they saw more of their children, but mothers were more depressed because they still had the burden of housework (Lyttelton, Zang, and Musick 2020). So where there was some evidence of greater gender equality, there were predictions of a positive outcome of the pandemic (Wiest 2020). But other reports of women losing jobs or dropping out of the workforce because of home demands pessimistically predicted long-term disastrous consequences for women's work participation (Alon et al. 2020a,b; Cohen 2020).

A serendipitous gender effect was that the leaders of countries that most successfully combated the coronavirus were women (Garikipati and Kambhampati 2020). Eight countries with the best outcomes of controlling cases and deaths all had women leaders whose actions were early and decisive. The countries were Bangladesh, Bolivia, Ethiopia, Georgia, Hong Kong, Namibia, Nepal, and Singapore. Also touted for their control of the spread of the virus were Jacinda Ardern, prime minister of New Zealand, and Angela Merkel, chancellor of Germany. At the beginning of June 2020, New Zealand was declared virus free (Cave 2020). However, other countries that hadn't controlled the coronavirus so well were also governed by women, so what was different about the successful women leaders?

A study comparing the COVID-19 death rates in US states with women and men governors found lower rates in states with women governors (Sergent and Stajkovic 2020). Even when men and women governors ordered early stay-at-home lockdowns at the same time, the states with women governors had lower death rates. A study of psychological leadership traits that were most effective in many crisis situations found that two traits came up consistently – empathy and confidence (Zenger and Folkman 2020). The authors of the study of women and men governors argued that these traits may generate greater compliance. And these traits, they found in analyzing speeches, were more often displayed by women governors.

Women's and men's leadership styles in the

COVID-19 crisis have been culturally different (Lewis 2020; Somvichian-Clausen 2020; Taub 2020; Wade and Bridges 2020). Men leaders are prone to using war metaphors, portraying the coronavirus as the enemy to be attacked aggressively and vanquished. More successful women leaders focused on communal efforts and careful planning that demanded shared long-term sacrifice, a leadership style considered "feminine." Clearly, comparisons need to be made within genders as well as between them. Women leaders are not all alike, nor are men leaders. Leaders of either gender can adopt effective "feminine" leadership styles.

Standpoint theory

Thirty years ago, the contention in medical and pharmaceutical research was that much of it left out women. The model body was male; women's bodies, with menstruation, menopause, pregnancy and childbirth, were seen as "deviant." In 1990, the Society for the Advancement of Women's Health Research was founded and has flourished with a journal (*Journal of Women's Health*) and ongoing research projects (Society for Women's Health Research 2020).

In the social sciences, a critique of gendered research is that it is not enough to just add more women to research teams or even to have them head a team ("add women and stir"); these women have to have a critical woman's viewpoint. Although men could certainly do research on and about women, and women on men, standpoint theory argues that women would be better able to design and conduct research from their own point of view (Harding 1991). But to make a difference they have to be critical of mainstream concepts that justify established lines of power, and they should recognize that "facts" often reflect stereotypical values and beliefs about women and men (Harding 1986).

Standpoint theory argues that as physical and social producers of children out of bodies, emotions, thought, and physical labor, women are grounded in material reality in ways that men usually are not. Women are responsible for most of the everyday work of living, even if they are highly educated, while highly educated men concentrate on the abstract and the intellectual. Because they are closely connected to their bodies and emotions, women's unconscious as well as conscious view of the world is unitary and concrete. If women produced knowledge, it would be much more in touch with the everyday material world and with the connectedness among people because that is what women experience.

Dorothy Smith, a feminist sociologist who has helped develop the ideas of standpoint theory, says that knowledge has to be sought in "everyday/everynight" local practices of individuals combined with institutional ethnography – mapping the practices of organizations and their members, which constrain individual actions by the relations of ruling. For example, research on marketing should go from the woman shopper to the organization of the store, the supply chain, means of production, and the global economy, recognizing that each level has hierarchal relations of ruling that impact on the people involved and that this impact is likely to be gendered (Smith 1987, 1990a,b, 2005).

While standpoint theory originally focused on the differences between women and men, it soon recognized that the gender categories were fragmented by other major statuses, especially racial and ethnic identity and social class (Collins 2000; McCall 2001). Their standpoints had to be made visible as well. Others argued for bringing "southern" theory into western thought. For Raewyn Connell (2007), the social experience and ideas that have emerged from Indigenous peoples and inhabitants of Australia, Latin America, India, Africa, and other postcolonial societies are sources of significant contributions to social science. Sandra Harding (1998) similarly argues for the importance of multicultural perspectives in science.

Standpoint theory was originally a bolster of the gender binary, arguing for major differences in outlook and behavior of women and men based on their different social locations in the gendered social structure. The later expansions of intersectionality and transnationalism argue for the value of perspectives of people from different social locations, not only gender (Collins 2019; Mohanty 2003). Ultimately, therefore, the gender binary actually fragmented as intersectionality superseded standpoint theory.

Hegemonic masculinity and the "new" masculinities

Parallel to feminist studies of women was the field of feminist studies of men. Most germane to explaining the persistence of the binary is the concept of hegemonic masculinity – elite men's pervasive dominance in values, knowledge, culture, and politics. Hegemony embodies the consent and compliance of subordinate men and women to the gender hierarchy; in other words, women's continued acceptance of the gender inequality of the binary and non-elite men allying with dominant men.

First proposed in Connell's *Gender and Power* (1987: 183–8), the concept was refined by Connell and Messerschmidt (2005) and later by Messerschmidt (2018), and Messerschmidt and Messner (2018). The 2005 critique reiterated the notion of multiple masculinities (hegemonic and subordinate) but, instead of compliance with gender inequality, pointed to antagonisms and resistances of subordinate men, especially over the issue of homosexuality. Gay men, formerly considered subordinate, began to filter into the ranks of the elite and to gain the acceptance of hegemonic men. Homophobia may have dropped out as part of heterosexual hegemonic masculinities but gender inequality has not, nor has racism.

While western hegemonic masculinity tends to be global (Connell 2005), there are regional and local variations. As social constructions, the variations allow for the possibility of change in what masculinities remain hegemonic and their downfall. Messerschmidt (2018) describes counterhegemonic practices that do not support gender inequality. In his research on adolescent boys, he encountered a group who were friends with girls, were non-hierarchical, and who walked away from bullies. They didn't reject masculinity but redefined it positively. "The boys aimed to be seen as boys as well as egalitarian in their gender relations, thus disrupting gender difference by redefining what it means to be a boy through the orchestration of positive masculinities" (2018: 144). They rejected hegemonic masculinity but continued to act within the binary.

These "hybrid masculinities" do not undermine hegemonic masculinity (Bridges and Pascoe 2018). White, middle-, and upper-class straight men strategically borrow elements of gay, Black, and working-class masculine styles and practices, but maintain their separate circles and hegemonic status. They sustain their power and privileges; their relationship to women is more protective than egalitarian. In some cases, men acknowledge the characteristics of hegemonic masculinity while deviating from them. A study of 24 men at an elite university found that while all agreed that for hegemonic men, academic achievement was downgraded in favor of athletics and social life, "nerds" who embraced concentrating on schoolwork nevertheless felt they were masculine as well (Gruys and Munsch 2020).

The #MeToo movement

The one recent major change in hegemonic masculinity is the #MeToo movement. Started by Tarana Burke in 2006 (Garcia 2017), women began to publicly reveal the extent to which they were sexually exploited and even raped by men with power over them for years in every field. The movement exploded in 2017 with Harvey Weinstein, movie mogul who had been paying off survivors of his sexual violence for years (Kantor and Twohey 2017). Ultimately, he landed in jail. Other accused men, instead of being protected by their male bosses, were fired and lost their good reputations (Farrow 2019). A review in 2018 of changes in laws, policies, and practices said, "Perhaps more than any new policy or law, the past year has been defined by a parade of once-powerful men resigning or being fired for sexual misconduct. In some cases, women are taking their place" (Greenberg 2018).

Not only the culture but the structure of workplaces has been changed to outlaw sexual harassment and exploitation (Greenberg 2018). Some of the changes at the US state level are banning nondisclosure or other confidentiality agreements as a condition of employment, expanding sexual harassment protections to independent contractors, volunteers, and interns, and mandating sexual harassment training and education. Companies are forced to disclose their history of sexual harassment suits and to attest to the fact that no managers, directors, or executives have been accused of sexual harassment. Men have stopped meeting women one-to-one behind closed doors and going on trips with just one woman for their own self-protection.

On US college campuses, women students have long complained that their reports of sexual assaults and rape were ignored. In 2011, then-President Obama's Department of Education's Office for Civil Rights sent a letter to 4,600 colleges and universities expanding Title IX, the 1972 law that prohibits sex discrimination in schools that receive federal funding. Sex discrimination earlier was expanded to include sexual harassment and assault. The directive shifted all belief to the accuser. The accused couldn't confront the accuser or belie the evidence against them. Also, sexual harassment was defined as "any unwelcome conduct of a sexual nature." While applauded for supporting traumatized women who claimed assault, the directive was criticized for denying the accused due process, even by feminists (Gertner 2015). In 2020, Education Secretary Betsy DeVos issued rules that gave more protections to the accused who faced discipline or expulsion due to allegations of sexual misconduct. The new directive was denounced by unions, the National Organization for Women, and Democratic senators as turning the clock back, but it was supported by some feminist legal scholars for restoring due process (Powell 2020). In comments on the DeVos decrees, Jeannie Suk Gersen (2020), a Harvard law professor, favored the option of informal resolution, such as mediation. Another good change was forbidding having one person act as investigator and judge, interviewing witnesses, examining evidence, and adjudicating the outcome. Suk Gersen notes that the definition of sexual harassment and the required response by school administrations was still fuzzy. The Obama regulations resulted in law suits and the DeVos rules are expected to also. Successful #MeToo accusations have generated reprisal lawsuits.

Sexual harassment and #MeToo accusations of sexual assault are rooted in the antagonism and power differences of the gender binary. Women standing up to men's sexual predations reinforce gender borders. Nonetheless, casual and violent sexual exploitation of subordinate women is no longer an assumed masculine privilege. While maintaining the gender binary, they have dropped out of the repertoire of hegemonic masculinity.

Gender-based violence

Outside of the workplace, gender-based violence proliferates. It includes bodily, sexual, and psychological violations and is embedded in the binary. Angela Hattery and Earl Smith (2019) argue that gender-based violence occurs when men have the power to create and sustain hegemonic ideologies of gender. They then use violence to monitor gender roles for cisgender women and gender boundaries for transgender women.

Violence can also be an expression of masculinity, especially in sports. If it is not exerted directly, as in boxing or US football, it is experienced vicariously in watching these sports (Messner 1992; Wacquant 2004). Part of the masculine embodiment in sports is to suffer pain as a rite of passage to manhood. Often, the ability to withstand body blows is flaunted as a mark of superiority to women. Ultimately, the ideological subtext of sports in western culture is that physical strength is men's prerogative, which justifies men's domination of women.

For boys on the cusp of becoming men, violence through hazing and "brooming" (anal rape with broom handles) and other physically demeaning rituals at the hands of slightly older men are very common (Brown 2021; Kimmel 2008: 95–122). They are ways of inculcating masculinity. To suffer and not complain or tell demonstrates that the boy is ready to move into the world of men.

All these forms of gender-based violence separate "manly" men from women and perpetuate the binary.

Sexuality and the binary

Sexuality and gender are both socially constructed and flexible over lifetimes (Gagnon and Simon 2005). They both encompass more than emotions and relationships – sexualities structure families and social lives. We have thought of sexuality as a binary like gender with only two categories, heterosexuality/homosexuality, but the realities of sexual variations have been recognized far longer than have current multiple genders. Heterosexuality, homosexuality, and bisexuality have distinctive structures, interactions, legalities, and cultural values (Greenberg 1988; Jackson and Scott 2010; Rust 2000). Yet they are embedded in the gender binary, which is much more limited in its variation. Gay men proclaim their masculinity with beards and burly bodies (Dozier 2005; Hennen 2005). Lesbians are first and foremost women in a continuum of emotional bonding (Rich 1980).

Statistics on homosexuality are notoriously slippery. Data questions may be based on sexual identity, behavior (number and frequency of same-sex partners), or attraction, which vary separately. A US study (Mishel 2019), based on interviews with 30,861 women and 24,357 men aged 15–45, found 4.9 percent of the women identified as bisexual and 1.5 percent as lesbian. Among the men, 1.9 percent identified as gay and 1.7 percent as bisexual. Combining the data on identity with the data on same-sex behavior and attraction, 20 percent of 6,277 women could be classified as lesbian or bisexual, and 10 percent of 2,470 men as gay or bisexual.

Lesbian, gay, and bisexual populations not only fluctuate separately over time but also by gender, social class, and racial and ethnic identity. A study using US General Social Survey data from 1988 to 2018 found steep increases over time in same-sex behavior by women and not as steep increases among men (Mishel, England, and Ford 2020). The women's rates especially rose with the sexual revolution loosening behavior. Among the men, the increase was greater for Black and working-class men. The authors speculate that gender norms regarding same-sex behavior are looser for women than white men, who have to uphold their superior status. Lower-status men have had increasing rates of incarceration and opportunities for same-sex sexual behavior, partially accounting for their increase in same-sex activity.

Bisexuality, which is usually combined with lesbian and gay sexuality, had a flurry of visibility and politics in the 1990s (Rust 1995; Tucker 1995). The politics concerned lesbians, who can be seen as betrayers if they sleep with a man. There is an ongoing academic quarterly, *Journal of Bisexuality*, which began in 2000 as an official journal of the American Institute of Bisexuality, which was established in 1998.

After a hiatus, bisexuality is now increasing in popularity. The US General Social Survey reported in 2018 that 3.3 percent of their responders identified as bisexual, compared to 1.7 percent who identified as lesbian or gay. When sexual identity was first included in GSS questions in 2008, only 1.1 percent identified as bisexual and 1.6 percent as lesbian or gay. Young Black women contributed the most to the increase in bisexual identification, with rates of 6–8 percent (Bridges and Moore 2018; Compton and Bridges 2019). Numbers of GSS responders fluctuate and can be small.

Does bisexuality support the gender binary? Yes, if the attraction is to (and sex with) both cisgender women and men. But if there are multiple genders, then there can be people who are attracted to queer and non-binary partners and any other gender. Since bisexuality as an identifying term assumes sex relations and attraction to two ("bi") genders, some in the community have adopted the term "pansexual" to indicate sex partners and attraction to all sorts of genders (Zane 2018). Pansexuality would be to binary sexuality what multiple genders are to the gender binary – part of the process of fragmentation.

Transgender and the binary

Transgender is a paradox when it comes to the binary. The transgender men described in the last chapter who menstruate, get pregnant, and give birth as men certainly upset the binary. So do the gender-rebellious children whose parents support their challenges to their birth-ascribed gender (Meadow 2018; Rahilly 2020; Travers

2019). Their refusal to abide by normative gender codes of names, clothes, hair length, sports, games, school bathroom use, and the myriad other aspects of gendered childhoods fragments the binary.

But completely exchanging gender identity ascribed at birth for the opposite gender as adults very much upholds the binary. The whole binary structure is what underpins being transgender since its goal is to trade one gender for the other. That means changing bodies and faces, clothing, hair, manner of speaking and walking and relating to others. Ultimately, it means changing one's status in the gender order. In-depth interviews with transgender men and women found that body transformation was interwoven with social presentation and sense of self as newly gendered. Transgender women described "retraining, redecorating, and remaking the body" in myriad small ways – walking and talking, dressing and using makeup, removing and restyling hair (Schrock, Reid, and Boyd 2005). Transgender men described growing facial hair and removing breasts as most important to establishing their new identity (Dozier 2005). But even large breasts can be masculinized as a glandular imperfection (Abelson 2019).

White transgender men, especially those who transitioned in secret, were very aware of their gain in status, noting that they received greater respect, authority, and attributions of competence (Schilt 2010). Often, they were compared as so much better than the "previous woman who had their job," who was of course, them. Black transgender men, however, lost status, reporting that they were harassed as gay or feared as threatening (Dozier 2005).

Catherine Connell (2010), in her in-depth interviews of 19 transgender men and women and genderqueer individuals, found that those who were "stealth" (hiding their transgender status) were most conforming to gender norms. Those who were open in their transgender status and genderqueer respondents tried to redo gender by mixing male and female self-presentations, but found that they "often felt they were gender disciplined and/or reinterpreted according to conventional gender norms" (2010: 39). Some transgender men did deliberately incorporate aspects of their former femininity, such as empathy, to counteract masculine privilege. The activist transgender people were more apt to challenge conventionally doing gender, but the resistance of others made it difficult to do gender differently. Connell says they are all "doing transgender" since they were very aware of gender inequality, having undergone reduced status for transgender women and enhanced status for transgender men.

The reinforcement of gender inequality is also evident in couples where cisgender women are living with transgender men. One study of 61 mostly white couples found that they tended to divide housework in conventionally gendered ways, with the woman doing most of it (Pfeffer 2017).

These couples, which were often previously lesbian relationships, also illustrate the gendered quality of sexuality. In some instances, the transitioning creates a heterosexual couple from one that was lesbian or gay, and in others the transitioning transforms a heterosexual couple into a same-gender relationship. The same partners may be involved but the gender of the sexuality has changed. Same-gender and different-gender sexualities have different qualities. Cisgender heterosexuals take that for granted but it is salient to couples involving a transgender person.

The pressure to maintain heteronormativity leads cisgender men to readily masculinize transgender men but cisgender women to reject them as potential sexual partners (Schilt and Westbrook 2009). In the women's eyes, such a relationship would be homosexual. For cisgender men, feeling they were tricked into homosexuality by a transgender woman who has male genitals can lead to violence, even murder, actions that restore the masculinity of the gender "normals."

In many ways, then, being transgender is made to fit into the binary to maintain heteronormativity (Westbrook and Schilt 2014). The gendering of transgender people is conventionalized, even to the point of reinforcing gender inequality and masculine privilege. The transgender people who resist and rebel against the binary need to find new ways of interacting with cisgender and transgender people. A study of controversies among transgender activists in Finland up to 1999 found resistance to medical categorization and treatment and rebellion against the binary (Wickman 2001). Seeing gender identity on a continuum ending with non-binary was one proposed solution as to where to fit transgender into the social order without reifying the binary. But for the most part, transgender people are today granted their preferred gender identity, with or without surgery and taking hormones, as long as they fit acceptable norms for gendered behavior and presentation of self.

Pros and cons of binary persistence

The areas of support for the gender binary are the myth of female and male brains, gendered research, standpoint theory, hegemonic masculinity and the "new" masculinities, the #MeToo movement, gender-based violence and gender-segregated sports, gendered sexuality, and the existence of transgender people. Not all have positive aspects.

I can't think of anything positive to say about the belief that brains can be codified as male and female and the conviction that from infancy they produce gendered behavior. Copious research indicates that human brains are not gendered. Further, brain structure and organization do not alone produce behavior, nor do genes or chromosomes or hormones. Human behavior is a composite of physical, environmental, and social influences. Also, gender differences at any age are minimal, so the effects that female and male brains are supposed to produce are inconsequential. Yet this series of beliefs – that brains are binary and produce binary behavior that creates and maintains the binary structure of our social world – is the foundation of western biological ideology. When the gender binary is seen as natural, it is also seen as immutable. When it is seen as socially constructed, it is seen as changeable.

Research that compares women and men is useful as an initial step in exploring a new area, as was shown with early data on COVID-19. It was found unexpectedly that men were more likely to get sick, to be sicker, and to die at higher rates than women. More expectedly, women were more likely to lose their jobs and, when they did work at home, to bear more of the burden of juggling childcare and home schooling. An unexpected finding was that countries where the pandemic was successfully controlled were likely to have women leaders.

This early data had to be disaggregated further. Race and ethnic groups, as well as economic inequity and crowded living conditions, were also shown to affect rates of coronavirus illness and death. The long-term effects of women's career erosion and imbalanced division of domestic labor were predicted to be dire. But there were data that indicated more involvement of heterosexual fathers in childcare when both partners worked from home. The data on women's leadership, when looked at further, showed that it wasn't gender but style of leadership that affected pandemic outcome. Leaders who demonstrated empathy and confidence generated more compliance with lockdown and mask wearing, resulting in lower levels of illness and death.

About thirty years ago, adding women to medical research was a positive step. In the social sciences and humanities, focusing on women's point of view, women's history, and women's cultural productions rectified the dominance of men's "gaze." Women's studies grew out of this turnaround, producing a prolif-eration of science, sociology, and history using women's standpoint. Past women's art, music, poetry, fiction, and plays were brought to the fore, as was contem-porary culture by women. Just as comparative gender research needs to be unpacked, research and culture that focused on women's point of view had to be inter-sected by other major factors – in particular, race and ethnicity. A whole genre of Black, Latina, and Asian women's studies has flourished.

The parallel area was the development of men's studies. It was diverse from the beginning, so we have data on men of all classes in many types of communities and in many countries. These studies were linked by the theory of hegemonic masculinity (and emphasized or complicit femininity), the analysis of the social hierarchy of dominant men and subordinate women. In this hierarchy, women are subordinate to the men of their class, race, ethnicity, religion, and place of residence. Except for actions to control physical, psychological, and sexual violence and its connection to sports, men's studies did not challenge the premises of the gender binary. In fact, they have examined the ways patriarchy is rooted in the ideology of two differentiated genders, one dominant and the other subordinate, without calling for dismantling the binary.

The gender-resistant #MeToo movement came out of feminism and wasn't incorporated into men's studies. It has been positive in encouraging women in many countries to accuse men they worked with of abuse ranging from commonplace sexual harassment to actual rape. The public outcry against accused men has resulted in many firings and reversals of iconic reputations. The negative side is countersuits and million-dollar buyouts. Another subtle negative side has been the realization among women that the men who have been revered as famous culture creators of the past were often guilty of sexual abuse. If they were to be ostracized, there would be no western culture left. Sexual abuse has been an intrinsic part of the hegemonic masculinity explored in men's studies. Both are rooted in the gender binary and its structure of dominance and subordination. It is clearly the downside of the persistence of the binary.

Even more detrimental to society is gender-based violence, bolstered by beliefs that men are legitimate upholders of conventional gender norms and gender borders, even when they use violence as a means of enforcement. Culturally sustaining gender-based violence are sports that rely on body-based violence. Such sports experienced vicariously become sources of masculinity, sustaining the binary. Detrimental to boys and men are bodily abuses that attack boys in the name of initiation to masculinity. These abuses inure boys to violence so that when they become men, they are prone to doing violence to women and boys to maintain their dominance.

The linkage of binary gender and patterns of sexuality has provided rich data in what has become an offshoot of gender studies – sexuality studies. Lesbians and gay men are not seen as separate from being women or men. Much of the sexuality literature explores their gendered communities. Same-gender marriages and families often emulate heterosexual patterns and so fit into the gender binary.

Being openly transgender is a proliferating and increasingly accepted phenomenon. Those transgender people who adopt conventionally gendered bodies, sexuality, interactions and identities confirm the binary. The downside is that they perpetuate gender inequality by accepting the diminishment or enhancement of status entailed by their transition from man to woman or woman to man.

Conclusion

The gender binary in western countries continues to be supported legally, interactionally, and structurally. Its major form of persistence is that it is the taken-for-granted default position. From birth, people are identified as male or female, dressed and brought up accordingly, interact with each other as members of their assigned gender, and are workers, family members, and often religious participants as women and men. In higher education, the military, space, and some religions, gender is officially deliberately ignored, although it informally emerges in discrimination, hidden biases, and sexual harassment of women.

Areas where the gender binary is still strong are gendered research, where gender is a standing variable, although now often fragmented intersectionally by social class, racial and ethnic identity, age, physical ability, and other major statuses. Feminists are ambivalent about the need to still stress women's accomplishments and standpoints to counter the assumptions of hegemonic masculinity about men's superiority. Patriarchal privilege – men's advantages in politics, the economy, and culture – is based on the gender binary. The continued social construction of gender differences is the scaffolding for inequalities between women and men. Beliefs that gender differences are natural, not constructed, legitimate discrimination, exploitation, and oppression of women as an inevitable outcome of the gender binary.

Sexuality seems to be one area where there is some blurring of the binary, particularly by bisexuals. Gay men and lesbians blur the binary by adopting heteronormative lifestyles, especially when married, Sexually, they stay within the binary. Transgender is built on the gender binary, with exchange of one gender identity for the other. The transgender non-binary individuals who change bodies but don't adopt new social identities certainly challenge the binary. The transgender women and men who embrace their new gender identities bolster it.

In the next chapter, I will explore why we don't have a gender revolution and the usefulness of degendering as an interim strategy that encourages continued fragmentation of the binary.

4

Why Haven't We Had a Gender Revolution?

Given all the people who fragment the gender binary in developed western societies, why haven't we had a revolution that tried to overturn the bi-gendered social structure? Why hasn't there been a concerted reaction against the structure of binary gender regimes and their legal and bureaucratic underpinnings? Why don't the gender non-conformists, non-binary people, intersex identifiers, and the menstruating and birthing men get together and revolt against the legal strictures of the binary? It may be that the very variety of gender challengers works against unitary political action and goals. For one thing, some gender rebels want more than two genders while others want to eradicate gender categories entirely.

Gender rebellious groups have had different goals to fight for. Gay men and lesbians need anti-discrimination laws and have battled for same-gender marriage. Transgender people want to be protected against discrimination but also want the legal right to change their birth certificates and names. Intersex identifiers are pushing against "normalizing" surgery. Non-binary people ask for legal X identifications, non-gendered titles, and neutral pronoun use. They are all fighting against the conventions of the gender binary but in myriad ways that preclude a concerted battle. They come up against the politics of identity.

The politics of identity

The politics of identity demand that you know who is "us" and who is "them." As William Connelly says in *Identity/Difference*, "Identity requires difference in order to be, and it conveys difference into otherness in order to secure its own self-certainty" (1991: 94). Gender rebels have to forge a visible identity to engage in concerted political action, as feminists have done.

Joan Wallach Scott calls it an inevitable feminist paradox that to fight to erase the effects of gender differences, you have to invoke them: "To the extent that it acted for 'women,' feminism produced the 'sexual difference' it sought to eliminate. This paradox – the need both to accept *and* to refuse 'sexual difference' – was the constitutive condition of feminism as a political movement throughout its history" (Scott 1996: 3–4).

Radical feminists in particular valorized women's ways – caring and emotionality – as equal to if not superior to men's focus on rationality and objectivity. Maya Maor (2015) found an example of such a practice in martial arts, where women teachers create their own more relational, emotional, and less brutal style of karate and tae kwon do to distinguish themselves from more aggressive men teachers. In the politics of identity, gender rebels run counter to feminists who feel the world isn't ready to drop the battle for women's visibility.

Particularly relevant to why the challengers of hegemonic gender identity don't achieve structural change is that acceptance and integration often produce what Urvashi Vaid (1995) calls virtual equality, the erasure of differences without changes in the social structure that make it possible to live differently. For the group, the marks of differentness may help their members identify one another as sources of help. As Suzanna Danuta Walters says of the gay and lesbian community in the United States, "One of the positive 'fallouts' of discrimination is the forging of community and the development of a concern for others, activism, a culture of responsibility. The response to AIDS is only one example" (2001: 19). However, Jane Ward's research (2004) on an AIDS service organization found that Latina lesbian women felt their healthcare needs were neglected because most of the money went to gay Latino men. Obviously, differences must be bracketed off for some political action and invoked when it is politically necessary to counter invisibility.

Many who queer the gender and sexuality binaries refuse to accept the structure of two and only two oppositional and fixed categories (Beemyn and Eliason 1996; Castro Varela, Dhawan, and Engel 2011; Elliot 2010). They contend that change will come when there are so many sexualities and genders that one cannot be played off against the other as normal and deviant, valued and stigmatized. Gender rebels construct ambiguities and blur borders, but they haven't undermined the structural or interactional foundations of gender as a binary institution. To make structural change, people with various unconventional gender identifications would have to coalesce into a unified force, confront conventional others in interaction, bring new knowledge to bear on gender issues, and insist on bureaucratic and legal recognition.

One problem is that those who eschew identity as either a woman or a man live in a borderland between women and men (Callis 2014). Another is that they consciously need to pursue the politics of power (Collins 2000: 275–90). Finally, they have to confront the pervasive interactive gender frame (Ridgeway 2011: 190–200). Let's look at each of the issues in turn.

Borderlands

As long as the gender binary persists, those without conventional gender identities live in a borderland. Drawing on the borderlands theory of Gloria Anzaldúa (1987) and the work of Pablo Vila (2000), April Scarlette Callis (2014) argues that people identifying as bisexual, pansexual, queer, and other sexual non-binary people inhabit the borderland between heterosexuality and homosexuality. Callis notes that theoretically, "borderlands simultaneously develop their own cultures while challenging hegemonic ideology" (2014: 68). By this analogy, those who inhabit sexual borderlands should be creating new forms of being sexual and eventually open a space for an institutionalized "third sexuality." What she found was the other way around: the sexual borderland was created by the structures of heterosexuality and homosexuality. The 37 people with non-binary sexualities that she interviewed "used 21 different terms or phrases in multiple combinations to label their sexual identities. Despite the wide array of labels used, all of these identities were formed as a reaction to the binary of heterosexual/homosexual, and each moved within and beyond this binary" (2014: 78).

Those denying and fragmenting gender identities similarly exist in a borderland constrained by a powerful binary frame. Like those with non-binary sexualities, those who invoke non-standard gender identities have not developed a shared identity or a culture. They include transgender people who alter their bodies in order to transition and live as women, men, or non-binary individuals, those with intersexed bodies who want a third gender or X identity, and those with the bodies they were born with who have adopted alternative gender identities. They are too heterogeneous to challenge the binary hegemony. In fact, some support the gender binary. Transgender people who want to pass as the gender they have transitioned into don't want to do away with binary genders. Intersexual people have generated substantial activism for the right to be accurately identified within the binary. They also don't want to do away with gender categories.

If people who are queering gender in one way or another did want to make a political difference, how would they get empowered?

The politics of empowerment

In *Black Feminist Thought*, Patricia Hill Collins (2000) says that to develop a politics of empowerment, you need to understand how power is organized and operates. According to Collins:

> Whether viewed through the lens of a single system of power or through that of intersecting oppressions, any particular matrix of domination is organized via four

interrelated domains of power, namely, the structural,
disciplinary, hegemonic, and interpersonal domains. . . .
The structural domain organizes oppression, whereas the
disciplinary domain manages it. The hegemonic domain
justifies oppression, and the interpersonal domain influences everyday lived experience and the individual
consciousness that ensues. (2000: 276)

How could those challenging the gender binary be
empowered to change it on each of the four dimensions
– structural, disciplinary, hegemonic, and interpersonal?

Queering gendering could affect the structure of the
binary if there were a concerted effort to either abolish
bureaucratic gender identities or to legally recognize
a range of them. Despite the biological challenges of
intersexed anatomies and anomalous hormonal and
chromosomal development, each body is forced into a
procrustean legal gender identity. Ambiguous infantile
genitalia are surgically altered to look "normal" soon
after birth (Dreger 1998; Kessler 1998). Anomalies
continuously plague gender categorization in sports,
resulting in forced body changes rather than challenges
to the intensely gendered structure of this powerful
and pervasive institution (Dreger 2009; Karkazis and
Jordan-Young 2014).

Collins (2000) notes the conflicts of "outsiders
within," those who have been able to move into
positions of power in dominant institutions but who
are in danger of cooptation to maintain their positions
and who therefore do not use their different perspectives to alter policies and practices. Transgender people
and gay men and lesbians have made their identities
visible and have promulgated nondiscriminatory laws,
legal identity change, and marriage equality, but just
adopting a variant gender identity is not universally

revolutionary. It seems to be a matter of individual consciousness – the end point of a process of change, not the beginning. After consciousness of the strictures of the two-gender social structure and the adoption of a gender-variant personal identity, there does not seem to be a path of rebellion against the whole gender regime. The two areas that should get shaken up by the open invocation and adoption of queer or non-binary gender identities are interpersonal interaction and new ways of thinking about gender. Are they?

The gender frame

Cecilia Ridgeway argues that to make gender less powerful as a frame for most interaction, people would have to stop automatically categorizing everyone they interact with as a man or a woman (2011: 190–2). She feels this is highly unlikely since it creates too much social confusion and even anxiety in others because it "challenges the stability and validity of their own identity as a man or woman" (2011: 191). Of course, if others' gender identity was irrelevant to the interaction, then no one's gender would be of consequence. For that to happen, gender status beliefs and relevance would have to alter substantially (2011: 193).

If men did more of women's work and women more of men's work both in the workforce and at home, Ridgeway argues, conventional gender beliefs would be challenged and gradually made less relevant. In actuality, what has happened is that when men do what has been conventionally seen as "women's work," such as nursing or childcare, it is reframed in gendered ways. Men in nursing do more physical work or get rapidly promoted to administrative positions. Men do childcare in masculine ways – roughhousing, sports, physical play. Women doing men's work, such as military combat, going into space, and ruling countries are seen as remarkable innovators, far from the norm. Women now dominate in previously masculine professions, such as western medicine, and have changed medical school curricula and ways of practice, turning much of it into women's work, but men still predominate in the more lucrative "masculine" specialties – surgery, neurology, and sports medicine. Thus gendered cultural overlays persist, even as practices have shifted to blur the boundaries between men's and women's enactment of them. Has there been structural change?

Towards gender equality

Gender as an institution is built on the construction of a gender binary and justifying differences between the genders. That allows for the subsequent hegemony of men and exploitation of women in low-paid work and unpaid domestic labor. The minimization of gender differences should lead to greater equality. If we can't tell or don't constantly remark on gender identity in face-to-face interaction, women and men would be social equals. I have argued that with that goal in mind, everyone should practice degendering – consciously act and talk and behave as if everyone had no gender (Lorber 2000, 2005). It could be everyone's revolution, not just those who deliberately queer gender. But it needs legal and bureaucratic degendering as well. In the more gender-equal countries, men and women are comparably educated, work in comparable occupations and professions for equal pay, have comparable political power, and share responsibility for the care of children.

These outcomes are supported by state and organizational policies, such as equal-pay laws and generous parental leave with pay for both men and women.

The World Economic Forum (2020) Global Gender Gap Index measures gender equality in the relative gaps between women and men in health, education, economy, and politics. According to the 2020 Global Gender Gap report, educational attainment and health and survival are close to parity in many countries – women and men share equally in whatever educational and health resources are available. The political empowerment gap has the greatest inequality at only 24.7 percent parity. The second-largest gap is in economic participation and opportunity; only 57.8 percent of this gap has been closed. Comparing countries, Iceland was the most gender-equal country in the world for the eleventh time in a row. It has closed almost 88 percent of its overall gender gap. Iceland is followed by Norway at 84.2 percent, Finland at 83.2, and Sweden at 82.0. The United Kingdom ranks 21st at 76.7. The United States ranks 26th at 75.6.

Do attitudes about gender norms match gender-equal outcomes? A recent global survey asked women and men in 24 countries to answer 10 questions about gender norms and expectations for men and women; the countries were ranked on the level of progressive gender attitudes. Matching the index of gender equality, the Nordic countries had the highest level of gender-neutral attitudes (YouGov 2015). In Sweden, there was very little difference between women's and men's attitudes. Thus the level of gender attitudes matches the level of gender equality in the economy and politics (Jackson and Jackson 2021). The connection could be that progressive gender attitudes affect whether people are likely to fight for gender-equal policies and laws.

How can progressive gender attitudes get routinely built into everyday gender-equal behavior as a basis for legal and bureaucratic change?

Producing gender-equal behavior

How can we produce more gender equality in our daily lives? We could demand gender-neutral bathrooms and language use. We could stop doing gender-reveal celebrations that feature the sex of a growing fetus and proclaiming it with pink or blue balloons, cakes, and fireworks. We could have a rainbow-colored gender-neutral celebration of the pregnancy instead. We could consciously seek out non-gendered clothing for small children and give them non-gendered toys and games. Since it's hard to find non-gendered toys, we could make sure children had some of each considered appropriate and not appropriate for their gender. We could insist that teachers throughout school grades do not separate and compare and contrast girls and boys but group them by other characteristics. Before puberty, girls and boys can do athletics together, and for older children there could probably be more gender-integrated teams or more concentration on gender-neutral sports.

For heterosexual couples, Ellen Lamont (2020) challenges them to date as equals if they intend to have an egalitarian marriage. She interviewed 105 college-educated young adults in the San Francisco Bay Area about their dating lives and romantic relationships and found that heterosexual women and men expressed a desire for permanent egalitarian relationships, where both partners have a career and share the labor at home. But they were still dating the old-fashioned gendered way

– the man asks for, plans, and pays for the date. When it comes time for a permanent commitment, the man is expected to be the one to propose marriage and present the woman with a ring. Lamont says that these rituals are viewed as romantic, chivalrous, and fun, but they actually lay the foundation for relationship inequality. Although her interviewees said they wanted shared marital practices, they were not likely to carry them out since they believed that men and women are innately different, with different interests, skills, and emotional availability. In contrast, the LGBQ respondents had egalitarian and flexible relationship practices from the beginning. One person wasn't responsible for asking for or paying for dates. They focused on communication, negotiation, flexibility, and building balanced relationships that took into consideration each person's needs.

Parenting in particular needs a gender-neutral approach. Describing revolutionary parenting, bell hooks (1984) said: "Structured in the definitions and the very usage of the terms father and mother is the sense that these two words refer to two distinctly different experiences. Women and men must define the work of fathering and mothering in the same way if males and females are to accept equal responsibility in parenting" (1984: 137).

Pregnancy, birth, and breastfeeding are often invoked as insurmountable barriers to men's parenting, seeming to give women bonding advantages that deepen their psychological leanings toward intensive mothering. Yet many men accompany the mother of their child to obstetric checkups, listen to the baby's heartbeat and look at the sonograms with the mother, take prenatal classes, coach the mother through the birth, hold the baby immediately after, and, even without paid parental leave, take time off from work after the birth. Many reports of shared parenting describe fathers waking up with the mother during night feeding and diapering and burping the baby, thus sharing the breastfeeding work and the bonding. Scott Coltrane (1996) was surprised by how many of the 20 co-parenting fathers he interviewed said it was "a rare opportunity to develop the sensitive, vulnerable, and caring parts of themselves. Many talked about discovering a new form of love and experiencing the world in different ways since they became fathers. Some also talked about how being a parent was helping them to work through unresolved emotional issues with their own fathers" (1996: 116–17). Men routinely sharing parenting would break the psychological cycle of gendering sons who grow up emotionally stilted and who have to learn parenting skills all over again.

Diane Ehrensaft (1987) claimed that the middle-class urban and academic heterosexual couples whom she studied shared parenting chores fairly equitably, but the mothers tended to take on more of the psychological and emotional management – to worry more. They felt they were on call for their children all the time while the fathers could let them cry. The mothers felt they had to struggle for separation, the fathers for closeness. Women, she said, *are* mothers; men *do* fathering. Yet in the course of fathering, the men had fallen in love with their children and wanted to be with them because they were so fascinating and lovable. The intensity of the men's feelings for their children reversed the conventional parental triangle; instead of the fathers being jealous of the time the mothers spent with the children, mothers felt left out of the father–child "couple."

For women and men, the skills of parenting are learned, usually "on the job." Expertise is the *result*, not the cause, of gendered parenting. If women are better than men at parenting, it's because they do it more.

Men who are single fathers or who do a significant amount of childcare become good at it, too. Barbara Risman (1987) interviewed men who became single parents out of necessity because their wives had died or left them with the children. These single fathers did not have previous beliefs about their capacity for intimate parenting, but they developed fully nurturing relationships with their children.

The right of men to parent had to be upheld legally in the United States. In 1975, in her pursuit of equal treatment under the law for women and men, Ruth Bader Ginsburg successfully defended a man whose wife died in childbirth and who wanted to be a full-time father to his newborn son (*Weinberger v. Wiesenfeld*). He had to go to court to be able to receive the social security benefits as a widower that a widow would be entitled to.

Sweden and Norway encourage men to share parenting with a "daddy month," paid parental leave that paralleled what mothers were getting. The days for fathers eventually were extended to months and years. But unlike mothers, fathers tended to break up their leave time into the equivalent of long weekends or extended vacations rather than spending intensive time after the birth of their child. These practices were condoned by peers and colleagues.

Degendering parenting entails downplaying conventional gender expectations. Fathers need to devote extensive physical and mental energy to their children while also earning a living, and mothers need to contribute substantial economic support to the family while also caring for and giving emotional attention to the children. Same-gender parents presumably don't have to go against the grain to the same extent since they have already challenged the gendered family structure, but gender norms about manhood and womanhood emerge even in same-gender households and have to be consciously counteracted (Malone and Cleary 2002).

Barbara Risman's study (1998) of shared parenting focused on deliberately "gender-fair" heterosexual families. An extensive search process turned up only 15 families that met the equality criteria: a 40/60 or better split on sharing household labor, equal responsibility for breadwinning and childrearing, and a self-assessment that their relationship was fair. Their gender-fairness was reflected in the surnames they used. They tended to divide housework by preference and competence without much discussion or argument (and with supplemental paid cleaning help). The majority of the couples had dual careers; both were career-oriented, and both felt that each other's career was equally as important as their own. Two of the couples were what Risman called "dual nurturers," less career-oriented than focused on home and family. Another family, with older children, was deliberately structured for sharing domestic tasks equally among all five members of the household.

Risman found that adults' relationships are often strengthened by their shared involvement with their children. They spend a lot of time talking about raising the children, comparing and improving each other's skills. Neither partner gets to have a conventional "male career" because neither has a "wife" to do the work at home. Both are workers in both spheres; both get the rewards of their work and of hands-on parenting. They also both get the fatigue, the boredom of performing household chores, the time crunch, the guilt that they are spending either too much or too little time with their children or on their work.

So if the goal is to maximize gender equality in daily life, there are many successful practices. Leaving personal gender queering aside, it is possible to maintain conventional gender identities but queer behavioral practices through concerted efforts at degendering. Thus a gender revolution can take place without an open confrontation over the gender binary.

Conclusion

The last two chapters indicate that the gender binary is both fragmented and persists. Except for intersectional research, the fragmentation is pretty much on the surface, with some non-binary self-presentations and pronoun usage and scattered legal recognition of X designations. The binary not only persists without acknowledgment of its ubiquity but is supported by routinely gendered research, continued belief in biological origins of gender differences, a focus on women's distinctiveness, and hegemonic masculinity. The gender binary is still built into most people's personal identity and self-presentation, organizes interactions, and structures the major components of the social order. The gender binary underlies western civilizations' value systems. Hegemonic masculinity, patriarchal privilege, and the gender binary are all part of each other. The dominance of the values and the culture of hegemonic masculinity asserting the superiority of men over women, and the legal structures and organizational policies that shore up the superior resources and power of men, depend on the gender binary and its elaboration of gender differences.

We are at a crossroads of fragmentation and persistence of the gender binary. If we continue with fragmentation, eventually doing away with gendered legal categories, identities, presentations of self, and social practices as "women" and "men," we will have the basis for equality – at least by gender category. Degendering would take us well along the road to doing away with gender differentiation and its consequence, gender inequality. Degendering assumes that sex is biological, physiological, and procreative, but not a good basis for social categorization; that sexual desire is fluid, not bound by gendered opposites; and that gender is no longer a valid way to organize societies. To the extent that gender is an institution, degendering breaks it down into its component parts and strips many of them of their binary structure. Gender identity, traits, competences, and behavior can be seen instead as spectrums with the "opposites" at either end. Gender is then no longer an institution.

But at the present time we still have institutional and interactional practices of gender inequality that have to be made visible and fought. And in order to fight gender inequality, we need to distinguish women from men as legal and social categories. We need to be able to compare them to make gender inequality visible.

That is the source of the new gender paradox. We need to persist with the gender binary, which is producing gender inequality, in order to fight it, and at the same time, fragment it more and more so it eventually disappears. A gender revolution is unlikely since the multiplicity of identities of the challengers of the binary and the variety of their goals makes united political action unfeasible. The various bi-gender challengers haven't recognized each other as allies, and the politics of identity needs a separation between us and them. They live on the borderland between the binary genders. If they did unite, it could create a third gender, yet many want to eschew gender identities entirely.

It may be that a gender revolution is not necessary to create gender equality. Both the multiplication and the minimization of gender identities have the potential of undermining the differential treatment of women and men. If we can't tell or don't constantly remark on who is what gender in face-to-face interaction, women and men become social equals. The more organizational policies, especially salaries and promotions, are equal for women and men, the less gender is relevant. With that goal in mind, everyone should practice degendering – consciously act and talk and behave as if everyone had no gender. It should be everyone's revolution, not just those who deliberately queer gender. But it needs legal and bureaucratic degendering as well as equitable organizational policies.

It would be revolutionary if birth certificates and ID cards and drivers' licenses did not indicate gender. The changes necessitated on marriage licenses by same-gender marriages are cases in point for how legal policies need to follow changed practices. Husbands and wives have become spouses. Equal sharers of childcare similarly should be parents, not mother and father. In many ways, degendering practices are revolutionary. Parents downplaying the gender of their children and men routinely parenting are revolutionary. So is gender-neutral treatment of children through the years of school. So is egalitarian dating. In many small ways, the gender binary can be chipped away by all of us.

What could be lost is the valorization of women and their history and accomplishments and the rich and varied women's cultures that feminists have worked so hard to produce, maintain, and make visible in the last 50 years. It would erase the "womanist" focus on the distinctive qualities of women – their relationship to their bodies and sexuality, their emotional and nurturing capabilities, and their special viewpoint in male-dominated societies and cultures.

In entering men's domains, women have had to emulate men. In parenting, men in turn are emulating women. To the extent that women's and men's leadership styles are different and women seem to have produced better outcomes in crises, such as the COVID-19 pandemic, men might emulate women in leadership, too.

A major social problem that degendering does not solve is violence against women – domestic battering and femicide – as well as sexual harassment, sexual attacks, and rape. The current ostracism of men who have routinely exploited and violated women and removing them from their positions of power has gone a long way to increasing women's ability to fight against their sexual vulnerability. But battling violence against women needs women to support other women. When they have downplayed their mutual gender, it's been a disaster. Women have assisted men in their sexual victimization of other women. More horrible, women family members in "honor" societies have killed daughters who they believe have destroyed family honor by sexual misdeeds or even by being raped.

In societies where women are more equal to men and where men's power and privileges have been diminished, it may be that maintaining the identity and visibility of women is not so necessary. Gradual degendering might eventually replace taken-for-granted gendered practices with degendered practices in bureaucracies and work organizations and in informal interaction in everyday life. But a period of self-conscious attention to gendering has to come first. You have to be aware of gendering to degender.

Our goal at present can't be a world without gender. Yet it needs to be a world without gender inequality.

And that takes both fragmentation *and* persistence of the binary. Breaking down the binary is needed in law, bureaucracies, politics, the economy, the culture, and other formal organizations to undermine discriminatory practices. But we need the binary to identify where formal gender inequality exists and to make hidden discriminatory practices visible. Perhaps the best epitaph for us is what Justice Ruth Bader Ginsburg wrote in her 1996 majority Supreme Court opinion that Virginia Military Institute should admit women. With the current understanding that most gender differences are socially constructed and not inborn, her statement in defense of eliminating gender discrimination but sustaining admirable gender differences holds for today: "'Inherent differences' between men and women, we have come to appreciate, remain cause for celebration, but not for denigration of the members of either sex or for artificial constraints on an individual's opportunity" (*United States vs Virginia et al.* 1996). Perhaps that is the best we can do in continuing to live with the gender binary while at the same time diminishing its invidious impact.

References

Abelson, M. (2019) *Men in Place: Trans Masculinity, Race, and Sexuality in America*. Minneapolis, MN: University of Minnesota Press.

Acker, J. (1990) "Hierarchies, jobs, and bodies: A theory of gendered organizations." *Gender & Society* 4: 139–58.

Acker, J. (1999) "Rewriting class, race, and gender: Problems in feminist rethinking," in M. M. Ferree, J. Lorber, and B. B. Hess (eds), *Revisioning Gender*. Thousand Oaks, CA: Sage.

Acker, J. (2006) *Class Questions: Feminist Answers*. Lanham, MD: Rowman & Littlefield.

Alon, T., Doepke, M., Olmstead-Rumsey, J., and Tertilt, M. (2020a) "The impact of COVID–19 on gender equality." *Covid Economics: Vetted and Real-Time Papers* 4: 62–85.

Alon, T. et al. (2020b) "This time it's different: The role of women's employment in a pandemic recession." https://faculty.wcas.northwestern.edu/~mdo738/research/ADOT_0720.pdf.

Anzaldúa, G. (1987) *Borderlands/La Frontera*. San Francisco, CA: Aunt Lute Books.

Baird, J. (2014) "Neither female nor male." *New York Times*, April 7.

Ball, A. L. (2014) "Who are you on Facebook now? Facebook customizes gender with 50 different choices." *New York Times*, April 6.

Barbee, H. and Schrock, D. (2019) "Un/gendering social selves: How nonbinary people navigate and experience a binarily gendered world." *Sociological Forum* 34: 572–93.

Baron, D. (2020) *What's Your Pronoun? Beyond He & She*. New York: Liveright.

Bauer, C. et al. (2018) "The 2016 Asexual Community Survey Summary Report." https://asexualcensus. files.wordpress.com/2018/11/2016_ace_community_ survey_report.pdf.

Beatie, T. (2008) *Labor of Love: The Story of One Man's Extraordinary Pregnancy*. New York: Seal Press.

Beemyn, B. and Eliason, M. (eds) (1996) *Queer Studies: A Lesbian, Gay, Bisexual and Transgender Anthology*. New York: New York University Press.

Bem, S. L. (1995) "Dismantling gender polarization and compulsory heterosexuality: Should we turn the volume down or up?" *Journal of Sex Research* 32: 329–34.

Bergner, D. (2019) "Neither/nor." *New York Times*, June 9.

Besse, M., Lampe, N. M., and Mann, E. S. (2020) "Experiences with achieving pregnancy and giving birth among transgender men: A narrative literature review." *Yale Journal of Biology and Medicine* 93: 517–28.

Blair-Loy, M. (2003) *Competing Devotions: Career and*

Family among Women Executives. Cambridge, MA: Harvard University Press.

Blaylock, R. (2020) "For linguists, it was the decade of the pronoun." theconversation.com, March 2.

Bolin, A. (1988) *In Search of Eve: Transsexual Rites of Passage*. South Hadley, MA: Bergin & Garvey.

Bourdieu, P. (1977) *Outline of a Theory of Practice*, trans. R. Nice. Cambridge, UK: Cambridge University Press.

Braidotti, R. (1994) *Nomadic Subjects: Embodiment and Sexual Difference in Feminist Theory*. New York: Columbia University Press.

Brassil, G. R. and Longman, J. (2020) "Who gets to compete in women's sports?" *New York Times*, August 19.

Bridges, T. and Moore, M. R. (2018) "Young women of color and shifting sexual identities." *Contexts*, Winter, 86–8.

Bridges, T. and Pascoe, C. J. (2018) "On the elasticity of gender hegemony: Why hybrid masculinities fail to undermine gender and sexual inequality," in J. W. Messerschmidt, P. Y. Martin, M. A. Messner, and R. Connell (eds), *Gender Reckonings: New Social Theory and Research*. New York: New York University Press.

Britton, D. M. (2000) "The epistemology of the gendered organization." *Gender & Society* 14: 418–34.

Brown, E. (2021) "Sexual assault against boys is a crisis." *Washington Post Magazine*, February 22.

Brown, P. L. (2005) "A quest for a restroom that's neither men's room nor women's room." *New York Times*, March 4.

Butler, J. (1990) *Gender Trouble: Feminism and the Subversion of Identity*. New York: Routledge.

Butler, J. (1993) *Bodies That Matter: On the Discursive Limits of "Sex."* New York: Routledge.

Butler, J. (2002) "Is kinship always already heterosexual?" *Differences: A Journal of Feminist Cultural Studies* 13: 14–44.

Callis, A. S. (2014) "Bisexual, pansexual, queer: Non-binary identities and the sexual borderlands." *Sexualities* 17: 63–80.

Carlson, D. L., Petts, R., and Pepin, J. R. (2020) "US couples' divisions of housework and childcare during COVID-19 pandemic." SocArXiv Papers, May.

Castro Varela, M. do Mar, Dhawan, N., and Engel, A. (eds) (2011) *Hegemony and Heteronormativity: Revisiting "The Political" in Queer Politics.* New York: Routledge.

Cavanagh, S. L. (2010) *Queering Bathrooms: Gender, Sexuality, and the Hygienic Imagination.* Toronto: University of Toronto Press.

Cave, D. (2020) "With no virus, New Zealand lifts lockdown." *New York Times*, June 9.

Chodorow, N. (1978) *The Reproduction of Mothering.* Berkeley, CA: University of California Press.

Clarey, C. and Kolata, G. (2009) "Gold awarded amid dispute over runner's sex." *New York Times*, August 21.

Cohen, P. (2020) "Recession's toll on women points to a lasting setback." *New York Times*, November 18.

Collins, C., Landivar, L. C., Ruppanner, L., and Scarborough, W. J. (2021) "COVID-19 and the gender gap in work hours." *Gender, Work & Organization* 28: 101–12.

Collins, P. H. (2000) *Black Feminist Thought: Knowledge, Consciousness, and the Politics of Empowerment* (rev. 10th Anniversary 2nd edn). New York: Routledge.

Collins, P. H. (2019) *Intersectionality as Critical Social Theory*. Durham, NC: Duke University Press.

Coltrane, S. (1996) *Family Man: Fatherhood, Housework, and Gender Equity*. New York: Oxford University Press.

Compton, D. and Bridges, T. (2019) "2018 GSS update on the US LGB population." Inequality by (Interior) Design, blog by T. Bridges, April 12.

Connell, C. (2010) "Doing, undoing, or redoing gender? Learning from the workplace experiences of transpeople." *Gender & Society* 24: 31–55.

Connell, R. (1987) *Gender and Power: Society, the Person and Sexual Politics*. Stanford, CA: Stanford University Press.

Connell, R. (1993) "The big picture: Masculinities in recent world history." *Theory and Society* 22: 597–623.

Connell, R. (1995) *Masculinities*. Berkeley, CA: University of California Press.

Connell, R. (1998) "Masculinities and globalization." *Men and Masculinities* 1: 3–23.

Connell, R. (2005) "Globalization, imperialism and masculinities," in M. S. Kimmel, J. Hearn, and R. Connell (eds), *Handbook of Studies on Men and Masculinities*. Thousand Oaks, CA: Sage.

Connell, R. (2007) *Southern Theory: Social Science and the Global Dynamics of Knowledge*. Cambridge, UK: Polity Press.

Connell, R. and Messerschmidt, J. (2005) "Hegemonic masculinity: Rethinking the concept." *Gender & Society* 19: 829–59.

Connelly, W. (1991) *Identity/Difference: Democratic Negotiations of Political Paradox*. New York: Cornell University Press.

Crenshaw, K. (1989) "Demarginalizing the intersection

of race and sex: A Black feminist critique of antidiscrimination doctrine, feminist theory and antiracist politics." *University of Chicago Legal Forum* 1989: 139–67.

Crouch, E. (2018) "Being non-binary in a language without gendered pronouns – Estonian." *Deep-Baltic*, March 20.

Cuthbert, K. (2019) "'When we talk about gender we talk about sex': (A)sexuality and (a)gendered subjectivities." *Gender & Society* 33: 841–64.

Darwin, H. (2017) "Doing gender beyond the binary: A virtual ethnography." *Symbolic Interaction* 4: 317–34.

Darwin, H. (2020) "Challenging the cisgender/transgender binary: Nonbinary people and the transgender label." *Gender & Society* 34: 357–80.

Davenport, C. and Beachum, L. (2019) "NASA's all-female spacewalk makes history: 'One giant leap for WOMANkind!'" *Washington Post*, October 18.

Davis, A. K. (2020) *Bathroom Battlegrounds: How Public Restrooms Shape the Gender Order*. Oakland, CA: University of California Press.

Davis, G. (2015) *Contesting Intersex: The Dubious Diagnosis*. New York: New York University Press.

del Giudice, M., Puts, D. A., Geary, D. C., and Schmitt, D. P. (2019) "Sex differences in brain and behavior: Eight counterpoints, disagreements and agreements on the origins of human sex differences." *Psychology Today*, April 8.

Devor, H. (1997) *FTM: Female-To-Male Transsexuals in Society*. Bloomington, IN: Indiana University Press.

Dozier, R. (2005) "Beards, breasts, and bodies: Doing sex in a gendered world." *Gender & Society* 19: 297–316.

Dreger, A. D. (1998) *Hermaphrodites and the Medical*

Invention of Sex. Cambridge, MA: Harvard University Press.

Dreger, A. (2009) "Seeking simple rules in complex gender realities." *New York Times*, October 25.

Ehrensaft, D. (1987) *Parenting Together: Men and Women Sharing the Care of Their Children*. Urbana, IL: University of Illinois Press.

Ekins, R. (1997) *Male Femaling: A Grounded Theory Approach to Cross-Dressing and Sex-Changing*. New York: Routledge.

Elliot, P. (2010) *Debates in Transgender, Queer, and Feminist Theory: Contested Sites*. Burlington, VT: Ashgate.

Epstein, C. F., Seron, C., Oglensky, B., and Sauté, R. (1999) *The Part-Time Paradox: Time Norms, Professional Life, Family, and Gender*. New York: Routledge.

Farrow, R. (2019) *Catch and Kill: Lies, Spies, and a Conspiracy to Protect Predators*. New York: Little, Brown.

Felski, R. (1997) "The doxa of difference." *Signs: Journal of Women in Culture and Society* 23: 1–21.

Ferguson, K. E. (1984) *The Feminist Case Against Bureaucracy*. Philadelphia, PA: Temple University Press.

Fine, C. (2010) *Delusions of Gender: How Our Minds, Society, and Neurosexism Create Difference*. New York: W. W. Norton.

Fine, C., Joel, D., and Rippon, G. (2019) "Eight things you need to know about sex, gender, brains, and behavior: A guide for academics, journalists, parents, gender diversity advocates, social justice warriors, tweeters, Facebookers, and everyone else," in R. Jordan-Young, G. Grossi, and G. Rippon (eds), *Scholar and Feminist Online* 15(2) (Neurogenderings).

Flax, J. (1987) "Postmodernism and gender relations in feminist theory." *Signs: Journal of Women in Culture and Society* 12: 621–43.

Ford, T. (2015) "My life without gender: 'Strangers are desperate to know what genitalia I have.'" Guardian. com, August 7.

Frank, S. E. (2020) "Queering menstruation: Trans and non-binary identity and body politics." *Sociological Inquiry* 90: 371–404.

Frye, M. (1996) "The necessity of differences: Constructing a positive category of women." *Signs: Journal of Women in Culture and Society* 21: 991–1010.

Gagnon, J. H. and Simon, W. (2005) *Sexual Conduct: The Social Sources of Human Sexuality*, 2nd edn. New York: Routledge.

Garcia, S. E. (2017) "The woman who created #MeToo long before hashtags." *New York Times*, October 20.

Garfinkel, H. (1967) *Studies in Ethnomethodology*. Englewood Cliffs, NJ: Prentice-Hall.

Garikipati, S. and Kambhampati, U. (2020) "Leading the fight against the pandemic: Does gender 'really' matter?" *SSRN*, June 3.

Gertner, N. (2015) "Sex, lies and justice: Can we reconcile the belated attention to rape on campus with due process?" *The American Prospect*, Winter.

Giddens, A. (1984) *The Constitution of Society: Outline of the Theory of Structuration*. Berkeley, CA: University of California Press.

Glenn, E. N. (1999) "The social construction and institutionalization of gender and race: An integrative framework," in M. M. Ferree, J. Lorber, and B. B. Hess (eds), *Revisioning Gender*. Thousand Oaks, CA: Sage.

Greenberg, D. F. (1988) *The Construction of Homosexuality*. Chicago. IL: Chicago University Press.

Greenberg, Z. (2018) "What has actually changed in a year." *New York Times*, October 6.

Gruys, K. and Munsch, C. L. (2020) "'Not your average nerd': Masculinities, privilege, and academic effort at an elite university." *Sociological Forum* 35: 346–69.

Hanna, A., Stevens, N. L., Keyes, O., and Ahmed, M. (2019) "Actually, we should not all use they/them pronouns." *Scientific American*, May 3.

Harding, S. (1986) *The Science Question in Feminism*. Ithaca, NY: Cornell University Press.

Harding, S. (1991) *Whose Science? Whose Knowledge? Thinking from Women's Lives*. Ithaca, NY: Cornell University Press.

Harding, S. (1998) *Is Science Multicultural? Feminism, Postcolonialism, and Epistemology*. Bloomington, IN: Indiana University Press.

Hattenstone, S. (2019) "The dad who gave birth: 'Being pregnant doesn't change me being a trans man.'" Guardian.com, April 20.

Hattery, A. J. and Smith, E. (2019) *Gender, Power, and Violence: Responding to Sexual and Intimate Partner Violence in Society Today*. Lanham, MD: Rowman & Littlefield.

Hennen, P. (2005) "Bear bodies, bear masculinity: Recuperation, resistance, or retreat?" *Gender & Society* 19: 25–43.

Herbenick, D. and Baldwin, A. (2014) "It's complicated: What each of Facebook's 51 new gender options means." *Daily Beast*, February 15.

Hochschild, A. R. (1997) *The Time Bind: When Work Becomes Home and Home Becomes Work*. New York: Metropolitan Books.

Hook, C. (2019) "Medicare figures show dozens of Australian men are now giving birth every year." Channel 7 News, August 8.

hooks, b. (1984) *Feminist Theory: From Margin to Center*. Boston, MA: South End Press.

Hosie, R. (2018) "Transgender male model fronts new period campaign." Independent.com, March 15.

Ingraham, C. (2006) "Thinking straight, acting bent: Heteronormativity and homosexuality," in K. Davis, M. Evans, and J. Lorber (eds), *Handbook of Gender and Women's Studies*. London: Sage.

Jackson, E. A. and Jackson, J. (2021) "Global perspectives on gender sensitivity and economic benefits," in W. L. Filho, A. M. Azul, L. Brandli, et al. (eds), *Gender Equality: Encyclopedia of the UN Sustainable Development Goals*. Berlin: Springer.

Jackson, R. M. (1998) *Destined for Equality: The Inevitable Rise of Women's Status*. Cambridge, MA: Harvard University Press.

Jackson, S. and Scott, S. (2010) *Theorizing Heterosexuality*. Maidenhead, UK: Open University Press.

Jacobs, J. A. (1989) *Revolving Doors: Sex Segregation and Women's Careers*. Stanford, CA: Stanford University Press.

James, S. E. et al. (2016) "Report of the 2015 US Transgender Survey." Washington, DC: National Center for Transgender Equality.

Joel, D. and Vikhanski, L. (2019) *Gender Mosaic: Beyond the Myth of the Male and Female Brain*. New York: Little Brown Spark.

Johnson, I. P. (2019) "Gender neutral wording is making German ridiculous, asserts association." DW.com, July 3.

Jordan-Young, R. M. (2010) *Brain Storm: The Flaws in the Science of Sex Differences*. Cambridge, MA: Harvard University Press.

Jordan-Young, R. and Karkazis, K. (2019) *Testosterone:*

An Unauthorized Biography. Cambridge, MA: Harvard University Press.

Kantor, J. and Twohey, M. (2017) "Sexual misconduct claims trail a Hollywood mogul." *New York Times*, October 6.

Karkazis, K. and Jordan-Young, R. (2014) "The trouble with too much T." *New York Times*, April 12.

Kersey, A. J., Csumitta, K. D., and Cantlon, J. F. (2019) "Gender similarities in the brain during mathematics development." *Science of Learning*, November 8.

Kessel, A. (2009) "Gold medal athlete Caster Semenya told to prove she is a woman." Guardian.com, August 19.

Kessler, S. J. (1990) "The medical construction of gender: Case management of intersexed infants." *Signs: Journal of Women in Culture and Society* 16: 3–26.

Kessler, S. J. (1998) *Lessons from the Intersexed*. New Brunswick, NJ: Rutgers University Press.

Kessler, S. J. and McKenna, W. (1978) *Gender: An Ethnomethodological Approach*. Chicago, IL: University of Chicago Press.

Kimmel, M. (2008) *Guyland: The Perilous World Where Boys Become Men*. New York: Harper Collins.

Kushner, A. (2019) "Why making Hebrew nonbinary is so crucial." *Forward*, January 24.

Lamont, E. (2020) *The Mating Game: How Gender Still Shapes How We Date*. Oakland, CA: University of California Press.

Lampe, N. M., Carter, S. K., and Sumerau, J. E. (2019) "Continuity and change in gender frames: The case of transgender reproduction." *Gender & Society* 33: 865–87.

Lewis, H. (2020) "The pandemic has revealed the weakness of strongmen." *Atlantic*, May 6.

Liptak, A. (2016) "Supreme Court blocks order allowing transgender student restroom choice." *New York Times*, August 3.

Liu, A. L., Shair-Rosenfield, S., Vance, L. R., and Csata, Z. (2018) "Linguistic origins of gender equality and women's rights." *Gender & Society* 32: 82–108.

Lodge, C. (2019) "Gender census," *Nonbinary Wiki*, March 31.

Longman, J. (2020) "Semenya's hopes of defending Olympic gold medal appear to end." *New York Times*, September 9.

Lorber, J. (1993) "Believing is seeing: Biology as ideology." *Gender & Society* 7: 568–81.

Lorber, J. (1994) *Paradoxes of Gender*. New Haven, CT: Yale University Press.

Lorber, J. (2000) "Using gender to undo gender: A feminist degendering movement." *Feminist Theory* 1: 101–18.

Lorber, J. (2005) *Breaking the Bowls: Degendering and Feminist Change*. New York: W. W. Norton.

Lorber, J. (2012) *Gender Inequality: Feminist Theories and Politics*, 5th edn. New York: Oxford University Press.

Lorber, J. (2018) "Paradoxes of gender redux: Multiple genders and the persistence of the binary," in J. W. Messerschmidt, P. Y. Martin, M. A. Messner, and R. Connell (eds), *Gender Reckonings: New Social Theory and Research*. New York: New York University Press.

Lyttelton, T., Zang, E., and Musick, K. (2020) "Before and during COVID-19: Telecommuting, work–family conflict, and gender equality." Briefing paper for Council on Contemporary Families, August 4.

Mackinnon, C. (1987) "Difference and dominance: On sex discrimination," in C. Mackinnon (ed.),

Feminism Unmodified. Cambridge, MA: Harvard University Press.

Magra, I. (2020) "British court rejects transgender man's appeal to be listed as a father." *New York Times,* April 30.

Malone, K. and Cleary, R. (2002) "(De)Sexing the family: Theorizing the social science of lesbian families." *Feminist Theory* 3: 271–93.

Maor, M. (2015) "How does practicing martial arts change women? And how do women change the practice of martial arts?" Presented at the Center for the Study of Women & Society, City University of New York Graduate Center, October 19.

Martin, P. Y. (2001) "'Mobilizing masculinities': Women's experiences of men at work." *Organization* 8: 587–618.

Martin, P. Y. (2003) "'Said and done' versus 'saying and doing': Gendering practices, practicing gender at work." *Gender & Society* 17: 342–66.

Martin, P. Y. (2004) "Gender as social institution." *Social Forces* 82: 1249–73.

McCall, L. (2001) *Complex Inequality: Gender, Class, and Race in the New Economy.* New York: Routledge.

Meadow, T. (2018) *Trans Kids: Being Gendered in the Twenty-First Century.* Oakland, CA: University of California Press.

Messerschmidt, J. W. (2018) *Hegemonic Masculinity: Formulation, Reformulation, and Amplification.* Lanham, MD: Rowman & Littlefield.

Messerschmidt, J. W. and Messner, M. A. (2018) "Hegemonic, nonhegemonic and 'new' masculinities," in J. W. Messerschmidt, P. Y. Martin, M. A. Messner, and R. Connell (eds), *Gender Reckonings: New Social Theory and Research.* New York: New York University Press.

Messner, M. A. (1992) *Power at Play: Sports and the Problem of Masculinity.* Boston, MA: Beacon Press.

Messner, M. A. (2002) *Taking the Field: Women, Men and Sports.* Minneapolis, MN: University of Minnesota Press.

Miller, C. C. (2020) "Moms and dads see split of lockdown chores differently." *New York Times*, May 7.

Mishel, E. (2019) "Intersections between sexual identity, sexual attraction, and sexual behavior among a nationally representative sample of American men and women." *Journal of Official Statistics* 35: 859–84.

Mishel, E., England, P., and Ford, J. (2020) "Cohort increases in sex with same-sex partners: Do trends vary by gender, race, and class?" *Gender & Society* 34: 178–209.

Moalem, S. (2020) "Why are so many more men dying from coronavirus?" *New York Times*, April 2.

Mohanty, C. T. (2003) *Feminism without Borders: Decolonizing Theory, Practicing Solidarity.* Durham, NC: Duke University Press.

Molotch, H. (1988) "The restroom and equal opportunity." *Sociological Forum* 3: 128–32.

Molotch, H. (2010) "On not making history," in H. Molotch and L. Norén (eds), *Toilet: Public Restrooms and the Politics of Sharing.* New York: New York University Press.

Nandi, J. (2013) "Germany got it right by offering a third gender option on birth certificates." Guardian. com, November 10.

Nentwich, J. (2004) *Die Gleichzeitigkeit von Differenz und Gleichheit. Neue Wege für die Gleichstellungsarbeit (The Simultaneousness of Difference and Sameness: New Ways for Equal Opportunities).* Königstein/ Taunus: Ulrike Helmer Verlag.

Nicholas, L. and Clark, S. (2020) "Leave those kids alone: On the uses and abuses and feminist queer potential of non-binary and genderqueer." *Journal of the International Network for Sexual Ethics and Politics*, Special Issue 3: 36–55.

Nossiter, A. (2019) "Guardians of French, deadlocked and griping." *New York Times*, March 4.

Packham, A. (2020) "Yes, mums are doing more chores and childcare than dads during lockdown." *Huffpost*, May 27.

Pfeffer, C. A. (2017) *Queering Families: The Postmodern Partnerships of Cisgender Women and Transgender Men*. New York: Oxford University Press.

Phoenix, C. H., Goy, R. W., Gerall, A. A., and Young, W. C. (1959) "Organizing action of prenatally administered testosterone proprionate on the tissues mediating mating behavior in the female guinea pig." *Endocrinology* 65: 369–82.

Politi, D. (2020) "Can the letter E change the world? A rising movement hopes so." *New York Times*, April 16.

Poster, W. R. (2001) "Dangerous places and nimble fingers: Discourses of gender discrimination and rights in global corporations." *International Journal of Politics, Culture and Society* 15: 77–105.

Powell, M. (2020) "Some feminist scholars say new assault policy is fair to the accused." *New York Times*, June 25.

Preves, S. E. (2003) *Intersex and Identity: The Contested Self*. New Brunswick, NJ: Rutgers University Press.

Rabin, R. C. (2020) "As women prove resilient to virus, trials test hormones on men." *New York Times*, April 27.

Rahilly, E. (2020) *Trans-Affirmative Parenting: Raising*

Kids across the Gender Spectrum. New York: New York University Press.

Reskin, B. F. and Roos, P. A. (1990) *Job Queues, Gender Queues: Explaining Women's Inroads into Male Occupations*. Philadelphia, PA: Temple University Press.

Rich, A. (1980) "Compulsory heterosexuality and lesbian existence." *Signs: Journal of Women in Culture and Society* 5: 631–60.

Richards, C., Bouman, W. P., and Barker, M. (eds) (2017) *Genderqueer and Non-Binary Genders*. London: Palgrave Macmillan.

Ridgeway, C. (1997) "Interaction and the conservation of gender inequality: Considering employment." *American Sociological Review* 62: 218–35.

Ridgeway, C. L. (2011) *Framed by Gender: How Gender Inequality Persists in the Modern World*. New York: Oxford University Press.

Rippon, G. (2019) *Gender and Our Brains: How New Neuroscience Explodes the Myths of the Male and Female Minds*. New York: Pantheon.

Risman, B. J. (1987) "Intimate relationships from a microstructural perspective: Men who mother." *Gender & Society* 1: 6–32.

Risman, B. J. (1998) *Gender Vertigo: American Families in Transition*. New Haven, CT: Yale University Press.

Rogers, M. F. (1992) "They were all passing: Agnes, Garfinkel, and company." *Gender & Society* 6: 169–91.

Rust, P. C. (ed.) (1995) *Bisexuality and the Challenge to Lesbian Politics: Sex, Loyalty, and Revolution*. New York: New York University Press.

Rust, P. C. R. (ed.) (2000) *Bisexuality in the United States*. New York: Columbia University Press.

Saguy, A. C. and Williams, J. A. (2019a) "Why we should all use they/them pronouns." *Scientific American*, April 11.

Saguy, A. C. and Williams, J. A. (2019b) "Reimagining gender: Gender neutrality in the news." *Signs: Journal of Women in Culture and Society* 44: 465–89.

Saguy, A. C., Williams, J., and Rees, M. (2020) "Reassessing gender neutrality." *Law & Society Review* 54: 7–32.

Saperstein, A. and Westbrook, L. (2021) "Categorical and gradational: Alternative survey measures of sex and gender." *European Journal of Politics and Gender* 4(1): 11–30.

Schilt, K. (2010) *Just One of the Guys? Transgender Men and the Persistence of Gender Inequality.* Chicago, IL: University of Chicago Press.

Schilt, K. and Westbrook, L. (2009) "Doing gender, doing heteronormativity: 'Gender normals,' transgender people, and the social maintenance of heterosexuality." *Gender & Society* 23: 440–64.

Schmidt, S. (2019) "A language for all: Teens in Argentina are leading the charge to eliminate gender in language." *Washington Post*, December 5.

Schrock, D., Reid, L., and Boyd, E. M. (2005) "Transsexuals' embodiment of womanhood." *Gender & Society* 19: 317–35.

Scott, J. W. (1996) *Only Paradoxes to Offer: French Feminists and the Rights of Man.* Cambridge, MA: Harvard University Press.

Sergent, K. and Stajkovic, A. D. (2020) "Women's leadership is associated with fewer deaths during the COVID-19 crisis: Quantitative and qualitative analyses of United States governors." *Journal of Applied Psychology* 105: 771–83.

Shattuck-Heidorn, H., Reiches, M. W., and Richardson,

S. R. (2020) "What's really behind the gender gap in COVID-19 deaths?" *New York Times*, June 24.

Smith, D. E. (1987) *The Everyday World as Problematic.* Toronto: University of Toronto Press.

Smith, D. E. (1990a) *The Conceptual Practices of Power: A Feminist Sociology of Knowledge.* Toronto: University of Toronto Press.

Smith, D. E. (1990b) *Texts, Facts, and Femininity: Exploring the Relations of Ruling.* New York: Routledge.

Smith, D. E. (2005) *Institutional Ethnography: A Sociology for People.* Lanham, MD: Rowman & Littlefield/AltaMira.

Society for Women's Health Research (2020) *Making Women's Health Mainstream: A History.* SWHR-30-Year-History-Book, https://swhr.org/about/history/timeline.

Somvichian-Clausen, A. (2020) "Countries led by women have fared better against coronavirus. Why?" The Hill.com, April 18.

Steinem, G. (1978) "If men could menstruate." *MS. Magazine*, October.

Suk Gersen, J. (2016) "The transgender bathroom debate and the looming Title IX crisis." *New Yorker*, May 24.

Suk Gersen, J. (2020) "How concerning are the Trump administration's new Title IX regulations?" *New Yorker*, May 16.

Tagliabue, J. (2012) "A school's big lesson begins with dropping personal pronouns." *New York Times*, November 14.

Taub, A. (2020) "Why are nations led by women doing better?" *New York Times*, May 16.

Tobia, J. (2015) "I am neither Mr, Mrs nor Ms but Mx." Guardian.com, August 31.

Travers, A. (2019) *The Trans Generation: How Trans Kids (and Their Parents) Are Creating a Gender Revolution*. New York: New York University Press.

Trinh, T. M. (1989) *Woman, Native, Other: Writing Postcoloniality and Feminism*. Bloomington, IN: Indiana University Press.

Tucker, N. (ed.) (1995) *Bisexual Politics: Theories, Queries, & Visions*. Binghamton, NY: Harrington Park Press.

United States v. Virginia et al. (1996) (94-1941) 518 U.S. 515.

Vaid, U. (1995) *Virtual Equality: The Mainstreaming of Gay and Lesbian Liberation*. New York: Doubleday Anchor.

Van den Wijngaard, M. (1997) *Reinventing the Sexes: The Biomedical Construction of Femininity and Masculinity*. Bloomington, IN: University of Indiana Press.

Varma, V. and Najar, N. (2014) "India's Supreme Court recognizes 3rd gender." *New York Times*, April 15.

Victor, D. (2020) "Machismo derails containment efforts." *New York Times*, October 12.

Vila, P. (2000) *Crossing Borders, Reinforcing Borders: Social Categories, Metaphors, and Narrative Identities on the US–Mexico Frontier*. Austin, TX: University of Texas Press.

von der Malsburg, T., Poppels, T., and Levy, R. P. (2020) "Implicit gender bias in linguistic descriptions for expected events: The cases of the 2016 United States and 2017 United Kingdom elections." *Psychological Science*, January 8.

Wacquant, L. (2004) *Body and Soul: Notebooks of an Apprentice Boxer*. New York: Oxford University Press.

Wade, L. and Bridges, T. (2020) "Why we need a 'feminine' economic reopening." *Gender & Society* blog, May 13.

Walters, S. D. (2001) *All the Rage: The Story of Gay Visibility in America.* Chicago: University of Chicago Press.

Ward, J. (2004) "'Not All Differences Are Created Equal': Multiple Jeopardy in a Gendered Organization." *Gender & Society* 18: 82–102.

Weinberger v. Wiesenfeld (1975) 420, U.S. 636.

Weiner, J. (2015) "The year of the toilet." *New York Times*, December 22.

West, C. and Fenstermaker, S. (1995) "Doing difference." *Gender & Society* 9: 8–37.

West, C. and Zimmerman, D. (1987) "Doing gender." *Gender & Society* 1: 125–51.

Westbrook, L. and Schilt, K. (2014) "Doing gender, determining gender: Transgender people, gender panics, and the maintenance of the sex/gender/sexuality system." *Gender & Society* 28: 32–57.

Wickman, J. (2001) *Transgender Politics: The Construction and Deconstruction of Binary Gender in the Finnish Transgender Community.* Abo, Finland: Abo Akademi University Press.

Wiest, B. (2020) "Women at the frontlines of COVID-19 might be starting the gender role reversal of the century." *Forbes*, April 17.

World Economic Forum (2020) Global Gender Gap Report. http://www3.weforum.org/docs/WEF_GGGR_2020.pdf.

Wortham, J. (2016) "When everyone can be 'queer,' is anyone?" *New York Times*, July 12.

Xiyi, W. et al. (2020) "Sex differences in severity and mortality among patients with COVID-19: Evidence from pooled literature analysis and insights from integrated bioinformatic analysis." https://www. researchgate.net/publication/340295228.

YouGov (2015) "Global Report: Attitudes to Gender." https://yougov.co.uk/news/2015/11/12/ global-gender-equality-report/.

Yuval-Davis, N. (1997) *Gender and Nation.* London: Sage.

Zane, Z. (2018) "What's the real difference between bi- and pansexual?" *Rolling Stone,* June 29.

Zell, E., Krizan, Z., and Teeter, S. R. (2015) "Evaluating gender similarities and differences using metasynthesis." *American Psychologist* 70: 10–20.

Zenger, J. and Folkman, J. (2020) "Women are better leaders during a crisis." *Harvard Business Review,* December 30.

Index

About the Author

Judith Lorber is Professor Emerita of Sociology and Women's Studies at the Graduate Center and Brooklyn College, CUNY. She received her Ph.D. from New York University in 1971 and began developing and teaching courses in women's studies in 1972. She was the Founding Editor of *Gender & Society*, official publication of Sociologists for Women in Society, and the first Coordinator of the CUNY Graduate Center's Women's Studies Certificate Program. She received the American Sociological Association Jessie Bernard Career Award for contributions to the study of women and gender in 1996.

She is the author of *Paradoxes of Gender, Breaking the Bowls: Degendering and Feminist Change, Gender Inequality: Feminist Theories and Politics*, and *Women Physicians: Careers, Status and Power*, as well as numerous articles on gender and on women doctors and patients. She is co-author of *Gender and the Social Construction of Illness* and *Gendered Bodies: Feminist Perspectives*, and co-editor of the *Handbook of Gender and Women's Studies, Revisioning Gender*, and *The Social Construction of Gender*.

September 2, 2021